A
Vision
of Jesus

Studies in Revelation One

To
Desmond and Mary

A
Vision
of Jesus

R. T. Kendall

Christian Focus

© R. T. Kendall
ISBN 1 85792 394 4

Published in 1999 by
Christian Focus Publications,
Geanies House, Fearn, Ross-shire,
IV20 1TW, Great Britain.

Cover design by Owen Daily

Contents

Preface

Just as I was preparing to write this Preface I was asked to do twelve daily devotional writings – on Revelation chapter 20! I have no idea what made the editor of that series think I was qualified to write on Revelation chapter 20 – the most controversial and difficult chapter in the Bible! I had to say no, because I don't understand it.

It may seem presumptuous even to write on Revelation chapter 1! But I see this as rather different, and it is something that I was drawn to many years ago. In fact one of my first series at Westminster Chapel on Sunday evenings was from Revelation chapter 1, and the result is the present book. I think some might have hoped I would go on after I finished that chapter, but I made it clear that I don't profess to understand the Book of Revelation! Not that I fully understand everything in Revelation chapter 1, but there is some hope that we have grasped a measure of the truth contained and implied in this glorious Book.

I want to thank Christian Focus for their continued trust in me and for inviting me to provide this book. Also I want to thank Margaret Downing for the editing of the material as well as Malcolm Maclean, with whom it is always a pleasure to work.

I dedicate this book to Professor and Mrs Desmond Burrows of Belfast – precious friends, God's gifts to Louise and me.

R T Kendall
Westminster Chapel, London
October 1999

1

Setting the Scene

Revelation 1:1

In recent years interest in the book of Revelation has been more carnal than spiritual, and I believe great harm has been done by those who have preached on it most, which is a pity. It has long been used as a way to excite people, focusing almost entirely upon interpreting signs and predicting future events. However, that is not the purpose of this book. I have no great eschatological theory to unravel, but rather, divorced from the sensational aspect that has often dogged interpretation of Revelation, I want us to explore its first chapter for our edification.

The book of Revelation was very popular in the 1960s, especially among the Jesus People, as we used to call them. You do not hear so much about them now. I remember attending a rock festival where the Rolling Stones were performing in Hollywood, Florida. Our church co-operated with other churches in giving out New Testaments. I noticed that those who accepted these, more often than not, were reading the book of Revelation (though not for the right reasons, I suspect). It was a time when people were experimenting with LSD and experiencing all kinds of drug-induced visions and dreams, and they would try to identify with the book. This is further reason for saying that interest in Revelation has often been more carnal than spiritual, and this has contributed to a natural reaction among many preachers and writers not to deal with the book at all.

As for my own ministry, I confess there has been a swinging of the pendulum. When I was a teenager, even before I felt the call to preach, I was greatly influenced by a pastor whom I loved, whose memory I still cherish. He often preached from the book of Revelation and had a huge chart predicting end-time events displayed on the walls of our church. He used this chart as a basis for his sermons on Revelation. These made a great impression on me, and I began to read one or two books that he recommended that supported his point of view. After I felt the call to preach and became a minister, I preached for almost the whole time on eschatology and prophecy and, not surprisingly perhaps, my sermons reflected the viewpoint of my former pastor. Later, I became a student at Trevecca College in Nashville, Tennessee, where I took a course on the New Testament. The professor took us through one book of the New Testament at a time, until finally, towards the end of term, he reached the book of Revelation. 'Now, students,' he said, 'we will deal with this book, but I want you to know, I don't understand it.' Then he added, 'Incidentally, is there anybody here who does?' Spotting my raised hand, he exclaimed, 'Ah, Mr Kendall! How would you like to teach the book of Revelation next Tuesday?'

'Sure,' I replied, and I did so. I expected that afterwards he would come up and congratulate me saying, 'That was tremendous!' Instead, he shrugged his shoulders and said, 'Well, I've heard that before.' This resulted in a swing of the pendulum, and for years I did not preach on Revelation at all. However, I think this was a mistake, and in this book I want to look at Revelation One carefully, for it has much to teach us.

I am convinced that the devil does not want us to

understand Revelation, for one of the most significant things about it is that it was the first direct word from Jesus to his church for more than sixty years. Think about this for a moment. Jesus died on the cross and ascended into heaven around AD 29 and the church began. (Its early history is described in the book of Acts.) Then around AD 50, inspired by the Holy Spirit, the first of the gospels, recalling the events and teaching of our Lord, emerged, as did the writings of the apostle Paul, which dealt mostly with doctrine. However, after that time Jesus did not speak *directly* to the church. Perhaps some believers wondered if Jesus had forgotten them. Christianity began to lose momentum to the extent that around AD 90 saw an increase in apostasy.

It was around this time that John was banished to the remote, uninhabited Isle of Patmos for preaching the word of God. While he was there, something happened to him. He says, 'On the Lord's Day I was in the Spirit, and I heard behind me a loud voice like a trumpet' (Rev. 1:10). From that point on Jesus himself speaks directly through John's vision. What Jesus says shows that he had not forgotten his church; on the contrary, he knew *everything* about it.

Likewise, Jesus knows everything there is to know about his church today. He knows what has happened in our lives; the things we dread, our concerns and anxieties. Sometimes he is silent for what might seem an eternity, but then, he suddenly appears.

Now, I want us to consider this question: What do the modern church, 'natural' (unconverted) humanity and the devil have in common? I believe there are three things they share.

First, they all had a good beginning. Think of the wonderful beginning of the church, with the resurrection of Jesus and the coming of the Holy Spirit on the Day of

Pentecost. These events were so real, so powerful, that not only were the disciples persuaded by them, but when they went out and testified publicly that Jesus was alive, more than three thousand people were also persuaded and were baptized. Despite persecution, the early Christians spoke with such authority that some Thessalonians once said that those 'who have turned the world upside down' were coming to their city too (Acts 17:6, AV). What a glorious beginning the church had!

But what about humanity? The Bible tells us this:

> Then God said, 'Let us make man in our image, in our likeness, and let them rule over the fish of the sea and the birds of the air, over the livestock, over all the earth, and over all the creatures that move along the ground.' So God created man in his own image, in the image of God he created him; male and female, he created them (Gen. 1:26-27).

> The LORD God formed the man from the dust of the ground and breathed into his nostrils the breath of life, and the man became a living being (Gen. 2:7).

So God created men and women in his image, moral, upright, innocent, having unblemished fellowship with him. Humanity had a glorious beginning too.

Did the devil have such a wonderful beginning? We know far less about his origin, but what we do know is that the devil once had an exalted position in heaven, and was known as 'Lucifer, Son of the Morning'. He too had a glorious beginning.

The second thing the modern church, 'natural' humanity and the devil all have in common is a fall.

It pains me to speak of the fall of the church, but I must. The apostle Paul knew it would happen. Believers in the Thessalonian church were so sure that Jesus' return was imminent that some were resigning from their jobs and selling their furniture and belongings. Paul got wind of this and (probably between AD 40 and AD 50) wrote to the church there, warning them not to be deceived, for before Jesus returned there would be a falling away from the faith and some would leave the church, seduced by spirits and devilish doctrines (2 Thess. 2: 1-12). He also said there would be a form of godliness but a form that denied its power (2 Tim. 3:5).

Thinking back across church history, it is clear there has been a series of falls, and in this sense history has repeated itself. The first great apostasy began between AD 90 and AD 100. We see another period of apostasy in the third and fourth centuries with the emergence of Arianism. God used a man named Athanasius to combat this heresy. Then, in the middle ages (or the dark ages as we sometimes call them) the Roman Catholic Church kept the people in ignorance and superstition until the advent of the great Reformation, when the Holy Spirit spoke to the church and there was a restoration of New Testament doctrine. Sadly, then another form of apostasy emerged, and this has been the pattern since: revivals followed by apostasy.

Humanity also had a fall. After God created Adam, he told him that he could eat the fruit of any tree in the garden except one. The Lord said, 'You are free to eat from any tree in the garden; but you must not eat from the tree of the knowledge of good and evil, for when you eat of it you will surely die' (Gen. 2:16-17). Then we read these sad words:

> When the woman saw that the fruit of the tree was good for food and pleasing to the eye, and also desirable for gaining wisdom, she took some and ate it. She also gave some to her husband, who was with her, and he ate it (Gen. 3:6).

As a result, God expelled them from the Garden of Eden and placed cherubim and 'a flaming sword flashing back and forth to guard the way to the tree of life' (Gen. 3:24).

Now the apostle Paul, who made such a great contribution to Christianity, tells us that when Adam sinned he took the whole human race down with him. He said that 'in Adam all die' (1 Cor. 15:22). You may say this is not true, but do you deny the wickedness that is in the world? Do you deny what is in your own heart and that doing wrong is easier than doing right? And ever since, men and women have been corrupt beings and have been kept from returning to the garden to reach up to the tree of life; God has kept men and women in their place, and those who partake of the fruit of that tree now do so at his invitation.

The devil also had a fall. Isaiah 14:12-14 speaks of this:

> How you have fallen from heaven,
>   O morning star, son of the dawn!
> You have been cast down to the earth,
>   you who once laid low the nations!
> You said in your heart,
>   'I will ascend to heaven;
> I will raise my throne
>   above the stars of God;
> I will sit enthroned on the mount of assembly,
>   on the utmost heights of the sacred mountain.
> I will ascend above the tops of the clouds;
>   I will make myself like the Most High.'

Jesus Christ described what he had witnessed. 'I saw Satan fall like lightning from heaven' (Luke 10:18). What a statement! Satan is now called 'the ruler of the kingdom of the air' (Eph. 2:2), 'the prince of this world' (John 12:31). Satan had a fall.

The third feature the modern church, 'natural' humanity and the devil have in common is that they all hate the book of Revelation.

Revelation is an embarrassment to the modern church because it transcends reason. God intended Christianity to be founded on *faith*. However, the modern church has felt the need to get people to see that there are good reasons for believing in God, and so, with the emergence of modern science, psychology and psychiatry, the church has been running to man and saying, 'Wait a minute, we can *explain*.' But when there is proof, there is no faith. The people of God are not those who have been persuaded by empirical evidence, but by faith. The book of Revelation cuts across reason and cannot be explained scientifically: it is apocalyptic. The word 'revelation' comes from a Greek word from which we derive the word 'apocalypse', meaning 'the unveiling of what is given'. Yet 'natural' humanity would much prefer to use its powers of deduction to obtain proof than to see what is given through the eyes of faith. The book of Revelation begins with the *revelation* of Jesus Christ. It is not something one can prove using logic or some scientific proof, one can only accept the revelation by faith.

Another reason that the modern church finds the book of Revelation so profoundly disturbing is because it so often speaks of the Lamb of God, who shed his blood for our sins. This has long been an embarrassment that it has tried to sweep under the carpet, calling this truth 'a myth'. However, Revelation confronts the modern church with the truth and it cannot deal with it.

Furthermore, Revelation keeps alive the idea of the second coming of Jesus – something the modern church would prefer not to think about, for it wishes to protect its conception of future events. Hence the emphasis on the social gospel – the idea that we are going to bring in the kingdom by what we do.

Moreover, the book of Revelation is an embarrassment to the modern church because it describes the eternal destiny of men and women as one of two places: heaven or hell. To the modern theologian, not only are these ideas too simple and lacking in sophistication, but the thought of hell awaiting unbelievers is an affront. The idea that God will punish sin is repulsive by nature. The entire book of Revelation, however, reveals God's justice, and does not fit the modern church's image of God. It would prefer a God it could manipulate and bend to its will, a God with whom it could be comfortable. But Revelation reveals the God of the Bible.

John said:

> I watched as he opened the sixth seal. There was a great earthquake. The sun turned black like sackcloth made of goat hair, the whole moon turned blood red, and the stars in the sky fell to earth, as late figs drop from a fig tree when shaken by a strong wind. The sky receded like a scroll, rolling up, and every mountain and island was removed from its place.
>
> Then the kings of the earth, the princes, the generals, the rich, the mighty, and every slave and every free man hid in caves and among the rocks of the mountains. They called to the mountains and the rocks, 'Fall on us and hide us from the face of him who sits on the throne and from the wrath of the Lamb! For the great day of their wrath has come, and who can stand?' (Rev. 6:12-17).

That is the God described in this book. 'Natural' men and women do not like a God like that.

Reason never brings people to God. In Chapter 16 John describes plagues and other terrifying happenings because of God's judgment on the earth, the very things that ought to have moved men and women to repentance. The Bible tells us that when the fourth angel poured out his bowl on the sun and people were scorched with heat, 'they cursed the name of God, who had control over these plagues, but they refused to repent and glorify him' (Rev. 16:9). Those things God sends to warn us ought to be the things that drive us back to him. But men and women who claim to want reason reject it after all. They regard Revelation, a book that reveals human depravity and reveals the God of the Bible, with hatred.

But what about the devil? It should not surprise you that he hates the book of Revelation. There are two reasons for this.

First, it shows us Satan's vulnerability. Now one *should* fear the devil, but only up to a point. My father used to say to me, 'Son, the devil is crafty; he is second only to God in wisdom and power.' That is true, but we should remember *he is second* and, thus, vulnerable. We can find out more about this in Revelation 12:11: 'They overcame him by the blood of the Lamb.' Satan hates and despises the blood of Jesus. When, in faith, we plead the blood of Jesus, the devil flees, defeated. This is why it is so important that we are persuaded of the power of Jesus' blood that was shed for us. Satan does not want us to understand this.

Second, Revelation is a book that shows the final chapter of the devil's biography: it reveals his end. Satan would much prefer us to believe that he does not even exist. If we do not believe in him, however, he has succeeded with us. The Bible tells us 'the god of this age has blinded the minds of unbelievers' (2 Cor. 4:4). So if we do not believe, it is not because we are clever or sophisticated but because we have been blinded to the truth. Yet through the power of his word God reigns supreme, and one day Satan, who would keep us in ignorance of our own eternal destination, will have an end when he is cast into the lake of fire.

Having seen why 'natural' humanity, the modern church and the devil all hate the book of Revelation, we should ask what is the right way to approach it. First we must abandon our eschatological biases. When we refuse to give up some cherished opinions with which we feel so comfortable, and which may, or may not, be true, we are so often robbed of our spiritual growth. When it comes to Revelation, many of us have our various traditions and may have read one or two books or heard one or two sermons and already have firm views. But if we read Revelation merely to have our opinions confirmed we should be careful, for the Holy Spirit will not penetrate our minds in such circumstances.

'What then, are we supposed to do?' you ask. 'What kind of presuppositions may we have?' My answer is only one: the persuasion that this book is the word of God. The Holy Spirit witnesses to this. All that is included in Revelation coheres with the great body of proof that this book is the infallible word of God. It tells us who God is, who we are, and how we can be saved. It tells us there is a heaven and a hell. It tells us all men and women will one day stand before God. On that day our only hope is that our names are written in the Lamb's book of life.

2

A Unique Revelation

Revelation 1:2

The book of Revelation belongs to the genre of apocalyptic literature. We find a small amount of this kind of writing in the Old Testament, especially in the books of Daniel and Ezekiel. In the New Testament, our Lord's discourse from the Mount of Olives in Matthew 24, Mark 13 and Luke 21 is sometimes called 'the little apocalypse'. But the book of Revelation is actually called 'The Apocalypse'.

As we saw in Chapter 1 the Greek word for 'apocalypse' means 'unveiling' or 'disclosure of what is hidden'. So 'apocalyptic' is an appropriate term to describe many breakthroughs in science and medicine; the discovery of penicillin, for instance, led to the development of many other antibiotics and saved thousands of lives. When such a breakthrough happens, there is a discontinuity with the past and the world is never the same again. The term 'apocalyptic' is also used in the study of history. Historians delving into events and characters of the past will sometimes discover some previously unknown fact that enables the world to see the event or character in a new light, and no one will ever see them in the same way again. This also happened, of course, throughout church history. Many great theologians, like Athanasius and Augustine, for instance, had great truths revealed to them that transformed the church. Another example is the Reformation, when there was such a disclosure of knowledge that it changed the course of human history.

Now the book of Revelation is commonly referred to as
'The Revelation of John', but it is not, in fact, about John,
although it tells us a little about him. Nor is it a revelation of
the church, although it gives us insight into the nature of the
church. Nor is it to be understood exclusively as the unveiling
of end-time events. Revelation reveals Jesus. This makes it
less interesting to some, but we cannot understand the book
until we accept it as it is meant to be – an unveiling of Jesus
Christ.

The timing of the book could not be accidental, coming,
as we noted in Chapter 1, as the first direct word from heaven
in almost sixty years at a time when there had been a great
falling away in the church as our Lord's comments
concerning the seven churches in Asia show (Rev. 2–3) and
church history also tells us. God addressed the problems in
the churches, but there is more to this book than that: it is
intended to give us an unveiling of the person of Jesus, a
true disclosure of himself as man and God, revealing both
why he came to earth and his purpose for his church.

One of the most significant things about Revelation is
that not only was it timely, but it is timeless. It has had a
meaning for each generation. Because of our natural tendency
to be introspective, most of us tend to apply this book in
particular directly to ourselves and the age in which we live.
I have met many people, holding various views on
Revelation, and it is interesting to hear that many believe
that the prophecy is going to be fulfilled almost immediately,
and some even think that it will be fulfilled in their own
town or city. I know some people back in Kentucky who
believe that when Jesus returns, he will come to their village.
Thinking parochially is natural for us. Yet there is something
to be said for it, because Revelation is written so that it has
a universal, timeless appeal; it can say several things to

different people and be right every time.

Take, for example, what the book meant to the early Christians, who were experiencing intense persecution. Having read Revelation 13, where there is a description of an antichrist, they had no doubt that Revelation was describing the Roman Empire. In Caesar, they clearly saw the one who spoke as God and was persecuting them. Martin Luther, on the other hand, had no doubt that the antichrist was the pope. He had good reason to think this, for he lived in an age when the Roman Catholic Church was keeping the whole of the western world in bondage and darkness. In the pages of Revelation God showed Luther what was happening, and after the Reformation the world was never the same again. We see in these examples how God can use its timeless quality and that it has been a source of comfort to those enduring persecution for their faith.

Do you know what it is like to be persecuted for being a Christian? Most of us don't. But this is not a good sign, for when Christianity flourishes in spiritual power there is always persecution. But in the West today there is little of that. There are countries where believers risk their lives to testify about Jesus and where God moves in power. The greatest risk we face is that someone will sneer at us or treat us with disdain. But I suspect that if God began to deal with us powerfully, then we too would see the emergence of real persecution. The book of Revelation is where the oppressed may come and identify with those who cried, 'How long, Sovereign Lord, holy and true, until you judge the inhabitants of the earth and avenge our blood?' (Rev. 6:10).

Is Revelation the infallible word of God? This question is very important, for if it is not then it is useless to us as a church. If it is, then we should plead for God to enable us to understand it because it is his word. We speak of an infallible

Bible, but there is a sense in which this book of Revelation has an admitted and self-conscious infallibility not always shared by other books of the Bible. For example, in his first letter to the Corinthians, Paul wrote, 'I speak this by permission, and not of commandment' (1 Cor. 7:6, AV). Paul had paused to give his own view and was leaving it up to us to decide whether to believe what he said. Then there is Peter's strange comment about Paul. He said, 'His [Paul's] letters contain some things that are hard to understand' (2 Pet. 3:16). By this, he meant we should think carefully about Paul's words because he says some things that could be misapplied by 'ignorant and unreliable people'.

Now there is no question at all whether those men spoke infallibly; they did. I simply want to show that the book of Revelation has an admission of infallibility that is unique. When John wrote his Gospel, he made it clear that he had been selective. In John 20:30 he wrote, 'Jesus did many other miraculous signs in the presence of his disciples, which are not recorded in this book.' At the end of his Gospel he says, 'Jesus did many other things as well. If every one of them were written down, I suppose that even the whole world would not have room for the books that would be written' (John 21:25). So John, no doubt inspired by the Holy Spirit, decided what he would tell. But the book of Revelation hems us in to accept an awareness of infallibility that is unique.

Why do I say this? For one thing, with two exceptions (I come to these in the next chapter), John expresses no opinion of his own. This book is not a theological discourse, but simply a description of what he saw. John was not well educated; he was a simple man, a fisherman by trade; he could never have concocted what is written here; all he did was to write what he saw. Interestingly, however, at one point he was forbidden to write what he had seen. 'And when the seven thunders spoke, I was about to write; but I heard a voice from heaven say, "Seal up what the seven thunders have said and do not write it down"' (Rev. 10:4). But he wrote down everything else he saw because he was given liberty to do so.

John did not hide his own infirmity; he let us see him as a man, and this adds greatly to the book's authenticity. In so many autobiographies the author paints a flattering image of himself, but the extraordinary thing about the Bible is that it portrays the *true* picture. In Hebrews 11, for example, we read of people who obtained a good report but who had done many things of which they would doubtless be ashamed, and yet God's record retained this. And so it is with Revelation, where we see John's own capacity for error when he attempted to worship the angel who came to him. 'At this I fell at his feet to worship him. But he said to me, "Do not do it! I am a fellow servant with you and with your brothers who hold to the testimony of Jesus. Worship God!"' (Rev. 19:10).

The second unique thing to note about Revelation is the claim it makes: it begins, 'The revelation of Jesus Christ, which God gave him to show his servants.' No other book in the Bible begins like this. Mark's Gospel, for example, just begins, 'The beginning of the gospel about Jesus Christ.' Paul's letters simply announce who he is; for example, 1 Corinthians begins: 'Paul, called to be an apostle of Christ Jesus . . .' But this book states its unique claim with its very first words: 'The revelation of Jesus Christ . . .'

> The revelation of Jesus Christ, which God gave him to show his servants what must soon take place. He made it known by sending his angel to his servant John, who testifies to everything he saw—that is, the word of God and the testimony of Jesus Christ (Rev. 1:1-2).

No other book in the New Testament so expressly claims to be the word of God. However, referring to the Old Testament, Peter does make this claim, for he says:

> Above all, you must understand that no prophecy of Scripture came about by the prophet's own interpretation. For prophecy never had its origin in the will of man, but men spoke from God as they were carried along by the Holy Spirit (2 Pet. 1:20-21).

Paul also makes a similar statement:

> All Scripture is God-breathed and is useful for teaching, rebuking, correcting and training in righteousness, so that the man of God may be thoroughly equipped for every good work (2 Tim. 3:16-17).

But nowhere, except in Revelation, does the New Testament so explicitly claim to be the word of God. We know, however, it was inspired by the Holy Spirit, for the Holy Spirit testifies to this; it speaks the claim of Jesus Christ; it is truly God speaking. But Revelation is expressly called 'the word of God'.

Moreover, this book came from Jesus in a way that is not claimed by any other book of the Bible. Now while we may deduce that other books came directly from Jesus Christ, they do not actually say this. But Revelation makes this unique claim. Looking again at Revelation 1:1-2, we read these words:

> The revelation of Jesus Christ, which God gave him to show his servants what must soon take place. He made it known by sending his angel to his servant John, who testifies to everything he saw—that is, the word of God and the testimony of Jesus Christ.

Furthermore, in the last chapter we read: 'I, Jesus, have sent my angel to give you this testimony for the churches' (Rev. 22:16). So if we need a direct word from Jesus, we have it here. This book, therefore, has an explicit claim to infallibility; even John's own theological view is absent.

The subsidiary proof that Revelation is the infallible word of God is that it coheres with the whole of the New Testament. It is simply descriptive: an apocalyptic vision given to John, who had no time to think it through, no time to question its theology; he wrote quickly so he could recall all he had seen. The degree to which Revelation coheres with the New Testament is a subject that could fill many chapters. I will just give you two examples.

First, consider the New Testament teaching that all have sinned and are in need of a Saviour. Paul's message was that all have sinned and the punishment for sin is death. He taught that Jesus lived a perfect life and died on the cross to satisfy God's justice. All the sin we have committed was laid on him, and he died in our stead. The vilest sinner can now be forgiven. In Revelation 5:1-6 John said:

> I saw in the right hand of him who sat on the throne a scroll with writing on both sides and sealed with seven seals. And I saw a mighty angel proclaiming in a loud voice, 'Who is worthy to break the seals and open the scroll?' But no-one in heaven or on earth or under the earth could open the scroll or even look inside it. I wept and wept because no-one was found who was worthy to open the scroll or look inside. Then one of the elders said to me, 'Do not weep! See, the Lion of the tribe of Judah, the Root of David has triumphed. He is able to open the scroll and its seven seals.'
>
> Then I saw a Lamb, looking as if it had been slain . . .

John did not impose his own theology; he wrote what he saw and heard, a message from Jesus cohering perfectly with

New Testament teaching: Jesus is the Lamb of God, sacrificed for us, the only one worthy to satisfy God's justice.

Let me give another example of the way John's vision is in accord with New Testament teaching. We learn there is a heaven. Jesus said, 'In my Father's house are many rooms; if it were not so, I would have told you' (John 14:2). In Revelation we have the correlation. John said, 'I saw the Holy City, the new Jerusalem, coming down out of heaven from God' (Rev. 21:2). Then he began to describe what would take place. 'He [God] will wipe every tear from their eyes. There will be no more death or mourning or crying or pain . . . ' (v. 4).

The wonderful thing about becoming a Christian is that not only are our sins forgiven but we have a home in heaven, a glorious hope, a glorious promise. Jesus, who takes all your sin upon himself, offers you eternal life. God's word is infallible and his promise is sure. One day I am going to that home Jesus is preparing for us (John 14:2). Will you meet me there?

3

The Unique Promise of the Book of Revelation

Revelation 1:3

In the previous chapter I said that John withheld his private views about Revelation but there were two exceptions. John's first personal comment is this:

> Blessed is the one who reads the words of this prophecy, and blessed are those who hear it and take to heart what is written in it, because the time is near (Rev. 1:3).

The other instance is in the last chapter where John says:

> I warn everyone who hears the words of the prophecy of this book: If anyone adds anything to them, God will add to him the plagues described in this book. And if anyone takes words away from this book of prophecy, God will take away from him his share in the tree of life and in the holy city, which are described in this book (Rev. 22:18–19).

So John, who, for the most part, wrote only what he saw in the vision, gave us these two comments: the first, a blessing promised to those who read, hear and keep the words of the prophecy, and the second, a warning.

In this chapter I want us to see the unique promise of this book. No other book in the Bible contains a promise like this: 'Blessed is the one who reads . . . '. The word 'blessed' is derived from a Greek word meaning 'happy'. Generally

25

the Bible does not speak in terms like this; nor does it often
encourage us to think that Christianity will bring us happiness
during our lifetime. Instead it tells us that we are to be holy:
'I am the LORD your God; consecrate yourselves and be holy,
because I am holy' (Lev. 11:44). The call to be holy is
repeated in the New Testament (Rom. 12:1; Eph. 1:4; 2 Tim.
1:9). Yet here in Revelation we see a formula, as it were, for
happiness. There is nothing quite like it elsewhere in the
Bible.

Happiness means being content with things as they are.
Some years ago I held a series of revival meetings in
Charleston, West Virginia and I remember being in a prayer
meeting and hearing an elderly Christian pray, 'O God, I
thank you that everything is *just* like it is.' He was truly a
happy man.

This promise ought to interest us all. 'Blessed is the one
who reads the words of this prophecy, and blessed are those
who hear it and take to heart what is written in it . . . '. Have
you ever heard a guarantee like this? People often make
pledges that they are unable to fulfil. For example, we hear
politicians promise us all kinds of good things, especially if
an election is looming. Yet suppose they kept their word, do
you think that would make everybody happy? But I can
promise that if everybody took these words in the book of
Revelation seriously, we would all be happy. I know of no
claim like this anywhere else.

The key words of the promise are 'reading', 'hearing'
and 'taking to heart'. 'Where's the catch?' you may ask. So
let us be fair and scrutinize this verse to see if there are any
hidden implications. It is a straightforward claim, so there
should be nothing to hide.

We begin by considering the word 'read'. 'Blessed is the
one who reads . . . '. Do you find happiness in reading? You

discover a measure of it perhaps when you find books on subjects that interest you. Perhaps you enjoy books about history, art, philosophy or psychology. Or perhaps you like novels or gossip magazines. A philosopher once said, 'Show me your books and I will tell you your need.'

Reading fulfils a need, so it is important. I have a friend in America who discovered this. He was in desperate straits and on the brink of suicide, but when he picked up a Bible and began to read, he found the Saviour he needed so desperately. His extraordinary testimony went something like this:

> 'I was only nineteen years old, but by that time I had made a complete mess of my life. I had tried everything to get out of the trouble I was in, but nothing worked and I was at my wits' end. I ended up in a hotel in New Orleans. Sitting in my room one day, in complete despair, I decided I had come to the end of the road and there was only one way out for me. I had a revolver in the chest beside my bed so I opened the drawer to take it out. Then I noticed a Gideon Bible there. For some strange reason I felt curious and thought, "Well, before I pull the trigger, I may as well look inside." So I took it out and began to read. I kept on reading: I couldn't put the Bible down. Later that day I got on my knees beside the bed and asked God's forgiveness for the past and committed my life to Jesus.'

That man is Dr. Carl Bates, who became pastor of the First Baptist Church in Charlotte, North Carolina and President of the sixteen million-strong Southern Baptist Convention. Reading the Bible fulfilled his need and it saved and changed his life. 'Blessed is the one who reads . . .'.

John may *hint* that reading is important, but he firmly *promises* that reading Revelation will bring blessing. Yet how many of us read this book? Many of us think the imagery it contains makes it impossible for us to grasp its meaning.

But we should not allow this to deter us, for the Holy Spirit has a way of taking God's word and applying it to our hearts and minds.

Now let us consider the word 'hearing'. Happy is he who reads and who hears! There are two ways in which we may hear the message of Revelation. First, we may hear it read aloud publicly. There can be little doubt that this was one way in which the early church heard it. At least seven copies of the text were made, because Jesus instructed John to give his vision to the seven churches in Asia (Rev. 1:11), so it was undoubtedly read aloud in each of these churches.

Second, hearing its message can also mean it forms the basis of preaching. At this point we should note that the Bible speaks of two kinds of hearing. To put it another way, we have two sets of ears. One set, of course, is our *natural* ears. Even before we are born, most of us are able to hear sound; although sometimes, as our physical faculties deteriorate with age, we may become deaf. The other set of ears is invisible, and contrary to the way it happens in life, we are *born* deaf. The fact is, our second set of ears do not pick up sounds and will not work unless the Holy Spirit enables us to hear in a new way. It is with this second set of ears, *spiritual* ears, that we hear God speaking to us.

It is wonderful when we hear with both sets of ears. Every minister knows what it is like to preach and find that people only hear with their physical ears. So all they think about during the sermon are the preacher's mannerisms, his oratory, his eloquence and his style. Sadly, that is all some ever take in.

I remember preaching in Fort Lauderdale, Florida, many years ago. One night I saw a man in the congregation whom I hoped had listened with his spiritual ears. Since I thought that I had preached with spiritual power, I went to him after the service, expecting him to be moved. But he simply looked at me, smiled and said, 'That was a really good talk.' That was all he received!

Bill Green, a friend of mine in the States, was a pastor of a church in New Jersey. He told me of an experience he had when he went to witness to a Jewish couple in their home. 'They were very polite,' he said, 'and took me into their living room. I opened my Bible and they listened to the gospel quietly with sober expressions. I talked for about half an hour and really believed I was driving my point home. Then the husband turned to his wife and exclaimed, "Listen to him. Isn't he terrific!" Next he looked at me and said, "You are just as good as Billy Graham! Mark my words: you will go far."' Poor Bill saw that he had made no impact at all. The couple had only heard Bill with their natural ears.

It was to the second set of ears – our spiritual ears – Jesus referred in the Parable of the Sower when he said, 'He who has ears to hear, let him hear' (Mark 4:9). Then in Revelation 3:20 Jesus again spoke of our spiritual hearing when he said, 'Here I am! I stand at the door and knock. If anyone hears my voice and opens the door, I will come in and eat with him, and he with me.' But note, his promise is contingent upon the second set of ears being opened.

What happens, then, if your second set of ears are opened?

Well, first, you find that instead of merely concluding that the minister was a good speaker, you suddenly think, 'He is speaking to my *soul*.' Until then you may have not even realized that you *had* a soul, but now you see that the preacher is dealing with things eternal and that the Holy Spirit has stopped you in your tracks. For a while you may feel deeply disturbed and unhappy. I have known of people who have found they could not sleep, and some have even felt they were losing their minds.

But now you begin to view life from a new perspective and to think about issues you have never considered before: the question of whether there is life beyond the grave, for example. As long as you heard only with your natural ears this question seemed merely academic, but once you begin to hear the Holy Spirit, you see that there *is* life after death and the Bible is serious about heaven and hell; you suddenly become aware that you are a sinner and that God could justly send you to hell.

At this point you have a choice.

One option open to you is to stifle your conscience, so maybe you bury yourself in the kind of books that you hope will contradict what you have been hearing, books on philosophy or psychology, for instance – anything to take your mind off your problem. Perhaps you find people who will comfort you and say, 'Oh, you are just feeling down at the moment. We all feel this way sometimes.' They tell you what you want to hear: that it's a passing phase. Or you may try to repress your guilt with alcohol, so you go to a pub and sit drinking until you can forget the notion that you have offended a holy God. That is *one* option you have after hearing the Holy Spirit speak to you.

However, there is another course of action you may take. Let us look at Revelation 1:3 again: 'Blessed is the one who reads the words of this prophecy, and blessed are those who hear it and *take to heart what is written in it* [my italics], because the time is near' (Rev. 1:3). The Greek word for 'take to heart' means 'mark attentively' or 'take heed'. This means that the message of Revelation is not mere opinion or mythology: what is said is *true*, so you must consider this whole matter most soberly; in fact, you must heed its message.

Now, as we have seen in an earlier chapter, the book of

Revelation belongs to the prophetic genre. 'Blessed is the one who reads the words of this prophecy . . .' (Rev. 1:3). Do you know what is meant by 'prophecy'? It is the disclosure of the divine will: the unveiling of what God is saying at a particular time.

The prophets emerge in the Old Testament. The first, and without doubt, the greatest of the Old Testament prophets was Moses. God gave him the Ten Commandments, and after these the Levitical laws. These laws constituted the will of God for Israel then and were all revealed through prophecy. After Moses came a series of prophets, among whom were Isaiah, Jeremiah, Ezekiel, Daniel, Hosea and Micah. There were also others, whose names are not written in the canon of Scripture. The message of the prophets was intended to persuade the Israelites to return to living according to God's Law and to warn them of the consequences of disobedience.

The message of Revelation is the unveiling of the divine will concerning Jesus Christ. This book tells you all you need to know about Jesus and all you need to know about yourself. Moreover, God has allowed us to participate in this prophecy. 'How can we do that?' you may ask. We participate when we respond by heeding its message: 'Blessed are those who hear it and take to heart what is written in it . . . '. The promise is to those who read, who hear and who obey.

The good news is that if you decide to heed the message of Revelation, you will not have to change your plans: you will not have to alter your marriage or become healthy. Nor will you have to act differently to qualify for the blessing. 'But,' you may say, 'surely I have to change; my life is in an awful mess.' But you cannot change yourself, for you are in bondage to sin. The help you need to do this must come

from an external source. I am not asking you to do something
that is, in fact, impossible for you to do.

You begin by agreeing with what the Bible says about
Jesus Christ, the Son of God. In Philippians 2:6-8 we read:

[Christ Jesus] . . .
being in very nature God,
    did not consider equality with God something to be grasped,
but made himself nothing,
    taking the very nature of a servant,
    being made in human likeness.
And being found in appearance as a man,
    he humbled himself
    and became obedient to death—
        even death on a cross!

The crucifixion, historically speaking, was a great tragedy.
It followed a mockery of a trial, which culminated in an
innocent man being condemned to death. But the Son of
God came into this world to die on the cross, and what
appeared to be a great disaster was, in fact, God's way of
dealing with our sin. You do not have to go to hell: you have
a way out when you agree with this book and do what it tells
you. Then you will become a member of the family of God
and co-heir with Jesus Christ (Rom. 8:17). Jesus will become
your solicitor and barrister rolled into one. And in taking on
your case, he will plead for you at the right hand of the Father
(Rom. 8:34). He knows all about you and your problems,
and he will work things out in a way that will exceed your
greatest hopes. God can take the broken pieces of your life
and make you whole.

4

Who is God?

Revelation 1:4–6

Who is God? What is he like? These questions have intrigued people throughout the course of history. However, many have denied his existence. In the nineteenth century the German philosopher Feuerbach said that God is nothing but man's projection on the backdrop of the universe. However, when I speak of God, I do not mean a God who exists only in one's imagination; I am talking about the *true* God. He is real: he exists: it is a question of getting to know him. Revelation tells us all we need to know about God; in fact John reveals his person in the first chapter:

> To the seven churches in the province of Asia:
> Grace and peace to you from him who is, and who was, and who is to come, and from the seven spirits before his throne, and from Jesus Christ, who is the faithful witness, the firstborn from the dead, and the ruler of the kings of the earth.
> To him who loves us and has freed us from our sins by his blood, and has made us to be a kingdom and priests to serve his God and Father—to him be glory and power for ever and ever! Amen (vv. 4–6).

In these few sentences John tells us who God is.

The kind of language he uses to describe God may surprise you, but even more astonishing is that it is *John* who speaks like this. Are you aware that he was once a simple fisherman?

He received no more than a basic education, and he gained what knowledge he had of the Bible through attending the synagogue and reading the Old Testament scriptures. Yet here, we find a man who had such a deep understanding of God. I find that encouraging; it gives me hope that one day I can understand God like that.

You may have many ideas about God and what he is like, but I want you to lay them aside and come with open minds to see what John says about him. I believe he shows us four things.

1. God is a triune being
In his greeting John confirms this:

> Grace and peace to you from him who is, and who was, and who is to come, and from the seven spirits before his throne, and from Jesus Christ, who is the faithful witness, the firstborn from the dead, and the ruler of the kings of the earth (Rev. 1:4-5).

When he says, 'Grace and peace to you from him who is, and who was, and who is to come', John is speaking of God the Father. 'The seven spirits before his throne' is God the Holy Spirit. It is not clear why John mentions seven spirits. I conclude that since the number seven is so often a number of completion throughout Revelation, John means the totality of the Holy Spirit. Moreover, some Bible students note seven references to the Spirit in Isaiah 11:2 and connect this with Revelation 1:4. And then he mentions Jesus, who is God the Son. So here, at the beginning of Revelation, is the doctrine of the Trinity: *one* God manifested in three persons. Now if you say, 'I don't understand that', I reply, 'Neither do I.' The Trinity is *above* reason: it cannot be explained by human logic. It is a teaching that we grasp only by faith.

However, when I say we grasp this doctrine by faith, I do not mean we take a chance. Let me explain. Some say, 'Well, I think I will try religion; I will *try* Christianity.' But they are only taking a gamble; they are not making a commitment because they believe. Faith is not a gamble; neither is it a leap, as some, influenced by existentialist notions, believe. To regard faith in this way would be rather like jumping across a wide chasm, hoping that somehow one will land safely on the other side. That is nonsense. No. Faith is a *persuasion* something is true; it is not something you can explain, yet you see it so clearly that it grasps you.

Here then is this man John, a simple man, not highly educated, nevertheless an intelligent man, who, along with the other disciples, espoused this mysterious teaching of the Trinity. How did they learn it? They certainly did not discover this teaching through studying philosophy: their understanding began with a person – Jesus of Nazareth.

Jesus was a historical figure: he really lived. The great Jewish scholar Josephus, writing in the first century, acknowledges the person and influence of Jesus. There is no doubt about this. There is early documentary evidence testifying to Jesus' existence. So what can we say about him? First, he was a man who time and again forgave sins. This was an extraordinary thing to do. The Jewish religious authorities, who witnessed this, were incensed and said, 'Why does this fellow talk like that? He's blaspheming! Who can forgive sins but God alone?' (Mark 2:7). Yet Jesus did. Not only did he forgive sins, but he promised rest to the weary. He said, 'Come to me, all you who are weary and burdened, and I will give you rest' (Matt. 11:28). Furthermore, he also promised to give eternal life. In John 5:24 Jesus said, 'I tell you the truth, whoever hears my word and believes him who sent me has eternal life and will not be condemned; he has crossed over from death to life.' Can you imagine anything more astounding than that? To promise these things is the prerogative of God alone.

However, many people believed Jesus. John, for one, was persuaded that what he said was absolutely true and so were many others. These people followed Jesus; they heard him preach and saw him heal the sick and raise the dead. They watched him die on the cross, and after his resurrection they saw him and spoke to him. Indeed, in just a few weeks, several thousand people were following him and claiming that Jesus was alive. So convinced were they that many died for their beliefs.

However, after his resurrection and ascension, these disciples began to see more of this man Jesus than they had grasped previously, because when God became man he laid aside his glory. There was nothing unusual in his appearance. Nobody who saw Jesus said, 'Oh, look, he must be God!' But now they saw that he was God in the flesh. When John recorded the things that Jesus did, he began his Gospel with these words: 'In the beginning was the Word [Jesus], and the Word was with God, and the Word was God' (John 1:1). So if we want to know who God is, we must begin with Jesus, and in his resurrection and ascension we see the ultimate truth: Jesus is God Incarnate.

While he was on earth Jesus had called God Father; he had prayed to his Father and claimed to have proceeded from his Father. Indeed he went as far as to say, 'Anyone who has seen me has seen the Father' (John 14:9). So now we can see that if Jesus is God and the Father is God, we see a new concept of God that was largely unknown to historic Judaism.

But before he ascended into heaven, Jesus taught his followers something else. We read in John 16:7 that he said, 'It is for your good that I am going away. Unless I go away, the Counsellor will not come to you.' He used the Greek word *parakletos* (we sometimes call the Holy Spirit, 'the Paraclete'); it is a Greek word that would probably have been better left untranslated so that it would take its own meaning. It means 'advocate', 'comforter', 'someone who comes alongside'. My point is this: when Jesus spoke of the *parakletos*, he equated him with himself. So here, he spoke about one who was the same as he. (You can read how the Holy Spirit came down and filled the disciples in Acts 2.)

Peter also equated God with the Holy Spirit. When he spoke to Ananias, who had lied to the apostles, he said, 'You have lied to the Holy Spirit. . . . You have not lied to men but to God' (Acts 5:3, 4). And as the church developed it began to see that God is manifested in three persons and it understood what Jesus meant when he said:

> 'All authority in heaven and on earth has been given to me. Therefore go and make disciples of all nations, baptising them in the name of the Father and of the Son and of the Holy Spirit, and teaching them to obey everything I have commanded you. And surely I will be with you always, to the very end of the age' (Matt. 28:18–20).

The early Christians adapted and incorporated the final sentence into a common benediction. Paul used it in his second letter to the Corinthians: 'May the grace of the Lord Jesus Christ, and the love of God, and the fellowship of the Holy Spirit be with you all' (2 Cor. 13:14). Today many churches still end the service with this blessing. Thus we see in part how the teaching of the triune God became known.

As I said earlier, the doctrine of the Trinity is above human understanding; we accept it by faith. We begin with Jesus, and as we understand who he is we see that he spoke the truth about himself, and we realize that it is the Holy Spirit who enables us to understand that we are dealing with a triune God.

2. God is eternal

The second thing John makes clear is that not only is God triune, but he is eternal. He put it like this: 'Grace and peace to you from him who is, and who was, and who is to come...'.

Now let us consider the first phrase: 'Grace and peace from him *who is* [my italics] . . .'. There is something happy about those words, something so peaceful and gracious. Do you know what it is to be treated unkindly? Do you feel no one understands you or wants your friendship? God understands; he wants you and he comes to you offering 'grace and peace'.

One German theologian was asked, 'What is the most profound thing you can say about God?' He thought for a minute, then he replied, 'That he *is*.' Thank God he *is*. When you are in trouble, great peace comes to you from him who is. Perhaps your life is in great turmoil and you feel there is no hope and nobody cares. Listen. God is there and he promises you his grace and his peace. Nobody else can make this promise: only the triune God, beyond our comprehension, can come to you and say, 'Grace and peace.'

Yet not only does he tell us he *is* but he tells us he *was*. 'Grace and peace to you from him who is, and *who was* [my italics] . . .'. That means before you were born he *was*, before creation and time began, before Satan and before the angels existed, God *was*. He has always existed; he is eternal.

But there is more: God says, 'Grace and peace from him who is, who was, and *who is to come* [my italics].' This is important: God is to come. After our lives are over, after the Judgment and after we have been in eternity for a million years, he is to come. God is eternal.

3. God is spirit

The third thing John saw was that God is spirit: he is not material; he is not a physical being. In fact, he is unlike anything in creation, for creation is matter. Now some believe that since God is essentially the Creator, there was never a time when he was *not* creating. This is nonsense. If you say that he was always creating, that means matter always existed. But the material universe and God are not co-eternal. We are dealing with almighty God who is spirit: he is totally independent of his creation. Jesus said, 'You have never heard his voice nor seen his form' (John 5:37). Indeed, one of the most intriguing passages of Scripture is Exodus 33 when Moses asked to see the glory of the Lord and God accommodated him to a certain extent, saying:

> 'I will cause all my goodness to pass in front of you, and I will proclaim my name, the LORD, in your presence. . . . But . . . you cannot see my face, for no-one may see me and live.'
>
> Then the LORD said, 'There is a place near me where you may stand on a rock. When my glory passes by, I will put you in a cleft in the rock and cover you with my hand until I have passed by. Then I will remove my hand and you will see my back; but my face must not be seen' (vv. 19–23).

Jesus himself said that God is spirit when he spoke to the woman at the well: 'God is spirit, and his worshippers must worship in spirit and in truth' (John 4:24). But we first learn that God is spirit at the very beginning of the Bible, in Genesis 1:2, which says that 'the Spirit of God was hovering over the waters'. This is the first evidence of the triune, eternal God.

4. God became a man

The fourth thing John shows us about God is something I have already mentioned: God became human.

> Grace and peace to you . . . from Jesus Christ, who is the faithful witness, the firstborn from the dead, and the ruler of the kings of the earth.

Note that John describes Jesus in three ways: He is (1) the faithful witness, (2) the firstborn from the dead, and (3) the ruler of the kings of the earth.

1. Jesus, the faithful witness

Let us look at the expression 'the faithful witness'. A witness is one who testifies to what he or she has seen. Have you acknowledged Jesus? If so, he has seen you do this for he is in heaven watching you; he knows everything about you, and he promised that if you acknowledged him before others, he would confess you before his Father (Matt. 10:32). What does it mean, then, that he is a *faithful* witness? It means that when you stand before God at the Judgment, you have nothing to fear. Jesus is the *faithful* witness and will keep the promise he made. He will say, 'Father, this person is mine.' Paul reminds us in Romans 10:11 that 'Everyone who trusts in him will never be put to shame.' Jesus is the faithful witness. He will not forget you or abandon you on the final day. Jesus promised, 'All that the Father gives me will come to me, and whoever comes to me I will never drive away' (John 6:37).

2. Jesus, the firstborn from the dead

Jesus has already experienced death and has risen from the grave in triumph. As the head of the family of God he went before us, and he has promised us that when the time comes for us to die, he will go with us (Psalm 23:4; Rom. 8:38-39). Not only that, but that you can face death confident that you will live with him for ever.

3. Jesus, the ruler of the kings of the earth.

Peter helps us to see the meaning of this phrase. In his first letter to the church he wrote, '[Jesus] has gone into heaven and is at God's right hand – with angels, authorities and powers in submission to him' (1 Pet. 3:22). So Jesus rules nations from a throne; he is indeed the 'ruler of the kings of the earth'. Jesus is Lord of lords and King of kings (Rev. 17:14). Someday he will come again and on that day Paul tells us that everyone will worship him:

At the name of Jesus every knee should bow,
    in heaven and on earth and under the earth,
and every tongue confess that Jesus Christ is Lord,
    to the glory of God the Father (Phil. 2:10-11).

5

How to Handle Guilt

Revelation 1:4–6

Sigmund Freud, the great Austrian psychiatrist, once said that guilt springs from the moment the parent begins to scold the child, who, taken aback by this abrupt change in parental behaviour, feels rejected. From that moment on, Freud asserted, the child continues to fear being rejected by the parent. This is the Freudian explanation of guilt. But it is not an adequate explanation, and today most psychiatrists have moved beyond this theory.

The theological explanation is that there are two causes for feelings of guilt: (1) sin has entered the world, and (2) we have a conscience. The story of the Fall of humanity proves this. In Genesis 3 we learn that God told Adam and Eve that they might eat the fruit of every tree in the Garden of Eden except from the tree in the middle of the garden, and if they disobeyed him they would die. But Satan, disguised as a serpent, persuaded Eve they might defy God with impunity. This is what happened next:

> When the woman saw that the fruit of the tree was good for food and pleasing to the eye, and also desirable for gaining wisdom, she took some and ate it. She also gave some to her husband, who was with her, and he ate it. Then the eyes of both of them were opened, and they realised they were naked; so they sewed fig leaves together and made coverings for themselves.

Then the man and his wife heard the sound of the LORD God as he was walking in the garden in the cool of the day, and they hid from the LORD God among the trees of the garden. But the LORD God called to the man, 'Where are you?'

He answered, 'I heard you in the garden, and I was afraid because I was naked; so I hid.'

And he said, 'Who told you that you were naked? Have you eaten from the tree that I commanded you not to eat from?' (Gen. 3:6-11).

The world has never been the same since sin and guilt entered it. But it is a fact that if we had no conscience, we would never feel guilty, or if there had never been sin, we would never feel guilty. However, because of these two combinations, guilt is with us. We have all experienced feelings of guilt to varying degrees. Have you ever driven down the motorway and heard the wail of a siren behind and seen that flashing blue light in your mirror? What a relief when the patrol car overtook you and sped away! It was not you the police were after.

When I was a boy in Ashland, Kentucky, I attended one school that had a public address system in every classroom. At the flick of a switch, the principal could speak to anybody in the building; he also had the option of tuning into any room and hearing everything that was going on. Sometimes, unexpectedly, he would turn on the microphone and clear his throat. Immediately my heart would start pounding. I was always afraid he would call my name and summon me to his office. Another thing I used to dread was taking my report card home. My throat would go dry and my heart would skip a beat when it was handed to me because I was afraid my grades would not be high enough to please my father.

It is almost impossible *not* to feel guilty about some things.

I feel guilty if I fail to buy a daily newspaper, and then I feel guilty if three days go by and I have not had time to read it.

Moreover, sometimes guilt can motivate us to do strange things when it comes to our relationships with others. For example, we may feel guilty because we dislike a person and to compensate we try to be extra friendly. We have all experienced guilt of this sort to varying degrees.

However, we should be aware that there are two kinds of guilt: true guilt and false guilt or pseudo-guilt. Paul Tournier, a Swiss Christian psychiatrist, in his excellent book *Guilt and Grace*, defined false guilt like this: 'False guilt is that which comes as a result of the judgements and suggestions of men.' All the illustrations I have used so far describe false guilt: the fear of how others might judge us. In fact, false guilt may motivate a neurotic person almost the whole time.

What, then, is true guilt? Again we turn to Paul Tournier for a definition: 'True guilt is that which results from divine judgements.' In other words, true guilt is the shame we feel when we have sinned against God.

But true guilt can only be truly experienced through regeneration. We may *try* to make unconverted people feel true guilt, but we never quite succeed in making them aware they have sinned against God: it is the Holy Spirit who does that. Before they become Christians, their guilt will be in terms of evading the consequences of their sin. But when the Holy Spirit convicts people of sin, they see they have offended God, and they come to the place where David was when he prayed, 'Against you, you only, have I sinned' (Ps. 51:4). Only a regenerate person can talk like that.

How, then, should we handle true guilt? I believe we have three options: (1) to take the 'fatal' solution, (2) to take the temporary solution or (3) to take the biblical solution.

1. The 'fatal' solution

Some people repress their guilt. They train their minds, sometimes consciously and sometimes unconsciously, not to worry about such feelings unduly and excuse their behaviour by saying, 'Well, what I did wasn't *that* bad.' Or they persuade themselves that they did nothing wrong at all and so they have no reason to feel guilty. Many of us deal with guilt in this way. Others have a different solution. They say, 'When you understand why you feel guilty, you will see you don't *need* to feel that way.' This is the psychoanalytic method.

In psychology there are three prominent schools of thought: (1) the psychoanalytic theory that began with Freud and continued with Jung, Adler and others; (2) behaviourist theories, popularized by the Harvard Professor B. F. Skinner, and (3) the humanistic theory promoted by Ronald May and Frederick Perls among others. However, all three contend that when you discover the reasons behind your guilt, you will see it is unnecessary.

The psychoanalysts would persuade you to call your conscience your 'super-ego'. They believe your super-ego was shaped by your childhood experiences, by the way your parents and other authority figures treated you, and since you are not responsible for this, you have no reason to feel guilty about the way you behave. However, there is much truth in this theory and I am not for a moment denying that help has been given to some who are seriously disturbed because of an over-working super ego. When people whose emotions have been damaged in this way are first converted, they are often disappointed to find that the miracle of the new birth has not caused all their guilt and anxiety to vanish. 'Surely,' they think, 'if I were *really* a Christian, I wouldn't have thoughts and feelings like these!' I cannot address this issue here, except to say that the psychoanalytic method can only go so far, but it can never reach the root of true guilt.

The central tenet of the behaviourist school of thought is that our actions are the result of our conditioning. They say people are biological machines and do not act consciously but *react* to external stimuli, rather like Pavlov's dog, which salivated when confronted by stimuli that preceded feeding. So the behaviourists conclude that guilt is a conditioned response and, therefore, is invalid.

However, the humanists and the existentialists go further than either the psychoanalysts or the behaviourists. They believe that a person must work out his own values and determine his own conduct. In other words he may do whatever seems right to him.

I will never forget that some years ago a psychologist friend invited me to attend an annual meeting of the American Humanistic Psychological Society. I have never regretted going because I learned so much. Nevertheless, with all respect, I must tell you that I witnessed some of the weirdest behaviour I have ever seen. Here they were at this meeting, 'actualizing their feelings'. Among the bizarre things I saw were people lying on the floor pounding it with their fists like five-year-old children in a tantrum!

However, I believe that if you take any one of these ideologies as the solution to the problem of true guilt it will be 'fatal', for if you deny the presence of guilt or if you rationalize or intellectualize it, it will distort you as a person, and inflict lasting damage. This is a point that I cannot emphasize too much.

Another thing that can happen if you deny guilt and continue doing what you want, without regard to what other people think and without regard to what God thinks, is that you will reach the point Paul describes in Romans 1:18–28 where God will simply hand you over to your sin and its consequences. Then you will have a reprobate mind – void of judgment and incapable of discerning truth from error and right from wrong. You may say, 'That will never happen to me.' Are you sure? When you, a person created in the image of God, play fast and loose with your conscience, there is no way you can escape the consequences. Moreover, you will not be aware of your condition.

The New Testament describes the consequences of ignoring our consciences. Paul put it to the Thessalonians like this:

> They perish because they refused to love the truth and so be saved. For this reason God sends them a powerful delusion so that they will believe the lie and so that all will be condemned who have not believed the truth but have delighted in wickedness (2 Thess. 2:10–12).

Those people never anticipated that God would do that to them. And, in his first letter to Timothy Paul warned that if people repeatedly reject the truth, their consciences will be seared 'as with a hot iron' (1 Tim. 4:2).

So denying or repressing guilt will not work. In fact, it may lead you to indulge in most bizarre behaviour, as we have seen, and sometimes it will have other undesirable results. For instance, it may cause physical illnesses like high blood pressure and insomnia; some psychiatrists believe it can even cause cancer. God created us in his own image and we ignore our conscience at our peril.

2. The temporary solution
However, when you begin to feel true guilt you may decide to take the second option – the temporary solution. So you say, 'I don't like feeling this way, but it is up to *me* to do

something about it. *I* can change my life and then I will have
no reason to feel guilty.' Thus you become the master or the
mistress of your fate. But making promises is only a
temporary solution, as I can testify. Many come to my vestry
to talk about the way to be rid of their guilt. Yet often, instead
of listening to what the Bible teaches, they say they will
avoid future temptation and promise to change their
behaviour. They go away feeling greatly relieved, but I know
that their resolve will last all of two days! It is so easy to
make a promise, but you will break it eventually. This
solution will only work for a time.

3. The biblical solution
The Bible offers a permanent solution to the problem of guilt.
But first you must recognize that God accepts you as you
are; he does not ask you to change. Then you need to
understand that simultaneously God pronounces the world
guilty and not guilty. This seems to be a paradox, so let me
explain.

The fact that sin entered the world is proved by our
feelings of shame. For had there been no sin, we would be
unable to feel guilty. But God created us in his own image
and he did not intend us to live in rebellion to him. The
Bible says that if we are not Christians he is angry with us
(Rom. 1:18) and we are under judgment (Rom. 6:23). 'But,'
you cry, 'you just said he loves us!' Yes, he does, as we see
when we read John 3:16: 'God so loved the world that he
gave his one and only Son, that whoever believes in him
shall not perish but have eternal life.'

Do you remember Freud's claim that guilt springs from
feelings of rejection? When you think of the implications of
this, you see this theory also demonstrates that people need
to feel loved. Perhaps your parents or a close friend have

rejected you (sadly, it happens), and because of this emotional damage you may find it difficult to believe that God loves you unconditionally. But it is true: he loves you and he accepts you just as you are.

Do you wonder how God is able to do that? We need to look at Revelation 1:5 for the answer: 'To him who loves us and *has freed us from our sins by his blood* [my italics].' You will remember I said earlier that God simultaneously pronounces us guilty and not guilty. But if God looks at our sin and says, 'Guilty!' how, then, could it be that we, who are sinners, are *not* guilty? The answer is simply because of what Jesus did for us when he shed his blood on the cross. The Authorised Version says that Jesus has 'washed us from our sins'. All our guilt was placed on Jesus when he took our place on the cross. And when we accept what he did for us and turn in repentance to him, God looks at us and his verdict is 'Not guilty!'

You may say, 'This is wonderful, but what must I do?' The answer is very simple. Look at verses 5 and 6:

> To him who loves us and has freed us from our sins by his own blood, and has made us to be a kingdom and priests to serve his God and Father — to him be glory and power for ever and ever! Amen.

God asks you to accept your role as a priest and as a member of his kingdom. That is a tremendous responsibility and means that you must live for him. You are no longer your own, for Jesus bought you with his blood (1 Cor. 6:19–20).

Finally, I want you to know that this will help you overcome the problem of false guilt. We saw earlier that false guilt springs from the fear of the suggestions and judgment of others. But Christians are not living for others, so they are not answerable to them; they are answerable to

God alone. God understands us and he is so patient; he is not a hard taskmaster (Matt. 11:28). Serving him is wonderful.

6

The End of the World

Revelation 1:7

No subject is more serious than this. Once only Christians asserted the world would end, often to the amusement of others around them. This claim became particularly laughable with the rise of the theory of evolution, which claimed that everything was improving as it evolved. However, recently attitudes have changed. Yet predictably, perhaps, contemporary theologians are saying very little about the end of the world. Many of them do not even believe in a final judgment and eternal punishment; instead they speak about the need for kindness and tolerance, about existentialism, and subjects like that. Strangely enough, it is *science* that is now predicting an end. Scientists base this belief not on the Bible but on the fact that so many countries of the world now have nuclear weapons. What happened in 1945 in Japan at Hiroshima and Nagasaki would seem negligible compared with what could happen if nuclear war broke out now.

I used to deliver newspapers when I was a boy, and one evening, a photograph of Albert Einstein on the front page caught my eye. Underneath bold headlines blazoned his warning that the world would end in a nuclear holocaust. Interestingly, he was not the first to predict a sudden, catastrophic end to life on our planet. You may be surprised to learn that almost two thousand years ago Peter described how the world would end like this:

But the day of the Lord will come like a thief. The heavens will disappear with a roar; the elements will be destroyed by fire, and the earth and everything in it will be laid bare.

Since everything will be destroyed in this way, what kind of people ought you to be? You ought to live holy and godly lives as you look forward to the day of God and speed its coming. That day will bring about the destruction of the heavens by fire, and the elements will melt in the heat. But in keeping with his promise we are looking forward to a new heaven and a new earth, the home of righteousness (2 Pet. 3:10-13).

But what do we mean when we speak of the end of the world? I am not speaking of physical death, which is a certainty for us all, unless Jesus returns first; neither am I speaking of the end of an era. I am talking about the moment when time as we know it will end and all material things will be dissolved. And since the Bible is God's word, we must look there to see what will happen.

The first thing to see is that the end of the world will be ushered in by the return of Jesus – the Second Coming. The church has looked forward to this event ever since the day Jesus ascended to heaven. Forty days after his resurrection Jesus took his disciples to the Mount of Olives and, after talking to them for a while, he was lifted up from the ground before their eyes until a cloud hid him from view. Acts 1:10-11 describes what happened next:

They were looking intently up into the sky as he was going, when suddenly two men dressed in white stood beside them. 'Men of Galilee,' they said, 'why do you stand here looking into the sky? This same Jesus, who has been taken from you into heaven, will come back in the same way you have seen him go into heaven.'

From that hour on, the church has expected that Jesus will come again; this is why we call it 'the *Second* Coming'.

John, who undoubtedly witnessed the ascension and heard this promise, describes how Jesus will return in verse 7. The first thing he said was 'Look, he is coming with the clouds.' This was John's way of saying that the return of Jesus will usher in the end of the world. Revelation speaks of this event again and again, and in a sense this is what the book of Revelation is about, although it is not the only important thing.

The Bible describes the phenomena that will accompany this event, but I must be candid with you and say that I do not understand them all. Perhaps we will not fully understand until we experience them. However, I would like to refer to two of them.

First, let us consider the 'clouds' John mentions in verse 7. Many other verses of Scripture speak of clouds accompanying Jesus' return (Dan. 7:13; Matt. 26:64; Mark 13:26; 14:62), but I will only talk about two. Here are the words of Jesus himself:

> 'At that time the sign of the Son of Man will appear in the sky, and all the nations of the earth will mourn. They will see the Son of Man coming on the clouds of the sky, with power and great glory' (Matt. 24:30).

The Scriptures speak of these clouds repeatedly. I don't know what they signify but I have heard various explanations. For example, some interpret the 'clouds' as clouds of angels, as so many will accompany Jesus on his return that it will seem as though there are clouds of them. But the choice of the word 'clouds' is no accident – it is used too often.

The second sign I want to show you that will herald the return of Jesus is 'the sound of a trumpet'. I do not understand

that either, but we often find it in scriptures dealing with the
Second Coming. In fact, Jesus speaks of trumpets in the very
next verse in Matthew 24:

> 'And he will send his angels with a loud trumpet call, and they
> will gather his elect from the four winds, from one end of the
> heavens to the other' (v. 31).

Paul also spoke of a trumpet call and said:

> Listen, I tell you a mystery: We will not all sleep, but we will
> all be changed—in a flash, in the twinkling of an eye, at the
> last trumpet. For the trumpet will sound, the dead will be raised
> imperishable, and we will be changed. For the perishable must
> clothe itself with the imperishable and the mortal with
> immortality (1 Cor. 15:51–53).

Paul mentioned this trumpet call again, in 1 Thessalonians
4:14–17:

> We believe that God will bring with Jesus those who have
> fallen asleep in him. According to the Lord's own word, we
> tell you that we who are still alive, who are left till the coming
> of the Lord, will certainly not precede those who have fallen
> asleep. For the Lord himself will come down from heaven,
> with a loud command, with the voice of the archangel and
> with the trumpet call of God, and the dead in Christ will rise
> first. After that, we who are still alive and are left will be caught
> up together with them in the clouds to meet the Lord in the air.
> And so we will be with the Lord forever.

We now come to the most miraculous thing of all, apart
from the Second Coming itself. Let us look at the second
part of Revelation 1:7. John says: 'Every eye will see him,
even those who pierced him; and all the peoples of the earth
will mourn because of him.' You may wonder how this will

happen. Well, there will be a resurrection of the dead. 'The sea gave up the dead that were in it, and death and Hades gave up the dead that were in them' (Rev. 20:13). Then every person who ever lived will see Jesus, including those men who nailed him to the cross.

Yet that is not all. The Bible says that the climax of this event will be the Final Judgment and that we will all be present 'great and small' (Rev. 20:12). Moreover, we learn there will be two classes of people there (Matt. 13:47–50; 25:46). The first class of people will consist of those who mourn because of him. (The Authorised Version says, they will 'wail because of him'.) But the second class of people will rejoice at the sight of Jesus. Those who wail lament because they know their destinies are sealed. Those who rejoice celebrate because they also know their destinies are sealed. However, the fate of both classes will have been determined before Jesus returns; nobody can be saved after the Second Coming takes place. There are two reasons for this.

The first is that faith will be impossible then, because faith is believing God without having empirical evidence that his word is true. Perhaps the reason you have not trusted God until now is that you say, 'I want proof. Show me *evidence* and I will believe it.' However, *faith* is believing God without evidence. But on that final day you will have proof, for 'every eye will see him'. Jesus will be there, so faith is no longer a possibility. Remember, there is only one way you can please God, that is by having faith and believing his word.

But there is a second reason that these people will wail: they will realize they have missed the opportunity of salvation. They will have no further chance, for it will be the *Final* Judgment; there will be no other court of appeal.

Have you ever heard a wail? I remember only hearing this awful sound once, when I was fifteen years old. One evening, as I was preparing to deliver my newspapers, I looked on the front page of *The Ashland Daily Independent* and saw that somebody I knew had been killed in the Korean war. He was only a year or two older than I was and had been the star basketball and baseball player of the Ashland Tomcats; he was one of my idols. When I finished my round, I went home and showed the report of his death to my parents, for his mother was a member of our church. They immediately said, 'We must go to her and see if there's anything we can do.' So we set off. But because so many others had also gone to see her, we had to park in the next block. When we got out of the car, although we were some distance away, we heard the most terrible, despairing wail coming from the house. When we went in, the mother took no notice of anybody, but just sat moaning incoherently. The time will come when all unbelievers will wail like that.

It is wonderful to have friends and relatives who support us when we are in trouble. When I was a boy, I knew I could always call on my father if I needed to feel secure. I remember when I was very small, I had to have an operation to remove my tonsils. Knowing I would be afraid, my father went into the operating theatre with me. I was terrified, and when they began to put the mask over my face to anaesthetize me, I began screaming at the top of my voice, 'Daddy! Daddy! Daddy!'

He said, 'I am right here, son. I won't leave the room.'

But at the Judgment there will be no one to comfort that group of unbelievers; they will stand alone to face God's wrath.

Yet for the second class of people at the Judgment it will be different, for this group will consist of those who believe

God's word. They will come from all walks of life and from all social classes, but this will no longer matter: it will not be a time when the famous are in the spotlight or when the rich have the prominence while the poor go unnoticed. What *will* matter is that these people believed the word of God and the Holy Spirit within them testified that it is true.

The return of Jesus will be no surprise to them: they will have eagerly expected his return. They will exclaim, 'It's wonderful! He has come. My destiny was sealed a long time ago when I took him at his word.' This group *will* have somebody there: the Lord Jesus Christ will be their witness at the Judgment and will plead for them. No doubt Satan would come forward if he had a chance and say to Jesus, 'You shouldn't let these people into heaven. I can show you all the things they have done.' But Jesus will stand before his Father and say, 'I prayed for them; I died for them, and they are mine.' We can be confident in this, because he said, 'Whoever acknowledges me before men, I will also acknowledge him before my Father in heaven' (Matt. 10:32).

This is why the thought of judgment does not terrify me and this is why John says, 'We will have confidence on the day of judgment' (1 John 4:17). I know my sins are sufficient to send me to hell (that is what I deserve). But I took God at his word when he said that those who believe on his Son 'will never be put to shame' (1 Pet. 2:6).

7

The Beginning of Eternity

Revelation 1:8

In the previous chapter I dealt with events that depict the end of the world, which will be ushered in by the return of Jesus. We saw that people will fall into one of two classes and that the reaction of each class of people at the sight of Jesus will be very different: those in the first class will wail because of him, while those in the second group will rejoice. The same event will thus cause opposite reactions.

The same was true when Jesus was on earth: nobody ever left his presence neutral: some loved him and some hated him. An example is the contrasting reactions of the two thieves who were crucified on either side of Jesus:

> One of the criminals who hung there hurled insults at him: 'Aren't you the Christ? Save yourself and us!'
>
> But the other criminal rebuked him. 'Don't you fear God,' he said, 'since you are under the same sentence? We are punished justly, for we are getting what our deeds deserve. But this man has done nothing wrong' (Luke 23:39–41).

These contrasting reactions typify those of the two classes of people at the Judgment, when some will wail and others will rejoice when they see Jesus.

Yet after the Final Judgment, what then? Revelation 1:8 describes the beginning of eternity. Jesus says:

'I am the Alpha and the Omega . . . who is, and who was, and who is to come, the Almighty.'

This verse parallels what happens immediately after the Judgment and parallels two verses in Hebrews:

Just as man is destined to die once, and after that to face judgment, so Christ was sacrificed once to take away the sins of many people; and he will appear a second time, not to bear sin, but to bring salvation to those who are waiting for him (Heb. 9:27–28).

If we believe it is true that everybody is 'destined to die once, and after that to face judgment', we will be eager to learn what will happen next. We find a clue in the words of Jesus I quoted earlier: 'I am the Alpha and the Omega . . . who is, and who was, and who is to come, the Almighty.' Alpha and Omega are the first and last letters of the Greek alphabet. These words describe who God is. Jesus was saying that he is the beginning and the end, the Lord of creation, the giver and withholder of knowledge.

Did you know that all knowledge comes from God and that he gives or withholds knowledge as he wills? We enjoy the benefit of many scientific, technological and medical developments, but we should remember we do so thanks to God's special grace and kindness to humanity. Yet science can only develop as far as God allows and human knowledge will never be complete.

This is not so with spiritual knowledge, which we begin to grasp when we become Christians. In Colossians 2:3 Paul reveals that in Jesus 'are hidden all the treasures of wisdom and knowledge'. The knowledge of Jesus Christ is *saving* knowledge that comes through the revelation of the Holy Spirit, and it is he who enables us to grasp who Jesus is and what he did; this knowledge, we call 'faith'. Imparting faith is the primary work of the Spirit.

Let us return to the account of the two criminals who were hanging on crosses on either side of Jesus. You will remember one hated him and one loved him. What made the difference? The difference was the Holy Spirit enabled one man to *see*. It is the Spirit who imparts faith, but it is in obedience to the command of Jesus, for it is he who gives eternal life. In John 10:28 he said, '*I* [my italics] give them eternal life.' Thus all knowledge, all revelation, stems from Jesus.

The most wonderful thing that ever happens is when Jesus reveals himself to a person. If it happens to you, then remember that he is bestowing on you an honour and a dignity higher than anything the world affords, for none other than the Son of God has revealed himself to you. He is the Alpha and the Omega, the Creator of all things, who gives or withholds knowledge, the one acknowledged in heaven as worthy of the highest praise.

Revelation 4:11 describes how the twenty-four elders fell down before God's throne and cried:

'You are worthy, our Lord and God,
    to receive glory and honour and power,
for you created all things,
    and by your will they were created
    and have their being.'

It is *he* who gives you life. You may think that you arrived in this world by some freak chance and that life has no purpose or meaning: things happen at random, there is chaos and you are a part of it and you conclude that when you die, you will be annihilated like any other animal. But God created you in his own image (Gen. 1:27) and he says, 'I gave you life and I put you on earth for a purpose.'

Yet God is not only the Creator, it is he who will bring all things to an end. Material things are not permanent. Life itself is transitory in nature: we meet friends for a while, and then we no longer see them. However, the ultimate thing to realize is that it will be God who will end all things and who will dissolve the whole of creation unto himself (2 Pet. 3:10).

However, *one* part of his creation will survive when the Judgment is over: that part made in his likeness. The human race is the pinnacle of God's creation; we are not plants; we are not just animals; we are men and women! And someday God will summon us to give an account of the way we have lived.

What will happen then? We find the answer in Revelation 20. We discover there that some people will die *twice*. Nobody disputes that we die once, but have you heard of the second death? In verses 11 and 12 John said:

> Then I saw a great white throne and him who was seated on it. Earth and sky fled from his presence, and there was no place for them. And I saw the dead, great and small, standing before the throne, and books were opened.

No matter how important we are or how insignificant – we will be there. *Everybody* will stand before God.

Verse 12 continues:

> Another book was opened, which is the book of life. The dead were judged according to what they had done as recorded in the books.

You may feel happy to read this and say, 'All I ask is that at the Judgment God will treat me with justice. I want God to judge me by my works.' You will get your wish: you will be treated with justice and you will be judged by your works.

Now 'works' here does not mean how efficiently and responsibly you have done your job. If that is your hope, I must tell you that God will judge your works by a far higher standard than that. But you may say, 'I want God to judge me on how well I have treated other people. I have never deliberately hurt anybody. I have tried to respect others and to do good whenever I had a chance, so I have no worries about the verdict at the Judgment.' But God will judge you by a far higher standard than that.

God is holy and he demands you reflect his holiness in your life (Lev. 11:44). However, when God created men and women in his own image, after his likeness, they sinned (Gen. 3), and from that moment on, nobody could reflect his purity and live without sinning. The truth is, your best is never good enough because so often it will be inspired by selfish motives. Indeed, the very fact that you want to be judged by your works and be saved by your own efforts shows your rebellion to God, because he sent his Son into the world to obtain your salvation.

What about the second class of people who will stand before God? Revelation 21:3 describes what will happen to them like this:

> I heard a loud voice from the throne saying, 'Now the dwelling of God is with men, and he will live with them. They will be his people, and God himself will be with them and be their God.'

You can see why they will rejoice. But there is more:

> He will wipe every tear from their eyes. There will be no more death or mourning or crying or pain, for the old order of things has passed away (v. 4).

These people will have much to celebrate.

But what will be the destiny of the first class of people at the Judgment? As I said earlier, God will judge these people according to their works. Revelation 20:14-15 reveals their destiny:

> The lake of fire is the second death. If anyone's name was not found written in the book of life, he was thrown into the lake of fire.

That is what will follow the conclusion of the trial. For those who are judged by their works will be found wanting. Nobody can produce the righteousness God demands. It is not enough simply to do your job well or to be kind to people; it is not enough to go to church and give generously to charity, for these very deeds are mixed with your unbelief. Your only hope of avoiding the lake of fire is that your name is written in the book of life.

You may ask how long the lake of fire continues to burn. I will answer with the words of God himself in Revelation 14:9-11:

> If anyone worships the beast and his image and receives his mark on the forehead or on the hand, he, too, will drink of the wine of God's fury, which has been poured full strength into the cup of his wrath. He will be tormented with burning sulphur in the presence of the holy angels and of the Lamb. And the smoke of their torment rises for ever and ever. There is no rest day or night for those who worship the beast and his image, or for anyone who receives the mark of his name.

That is the second death – this death means an eternal dying, for God created us in his own image, so we will never be annihilated. We are that part of creation which exists beyond the dissolution of matter into eternity, for we are special. Furthermore, the fires of hell do not satisfy God's justice, or the second death would be over in a flash. However, God sent his Son into the world with a specific purpose. Jesus shed his blood on the cross and satisfied the justice of God for ever. And those who go to heaven – those who will never see the second death – will be those who trusted that blood, for their names are written in the Lamb's book of life; they will number among those who will inherit the new Jerusalem coming down from God out of heaven (Rev. 21:1-4).

The last verse of 'Amazing Grace' says:

When we've been there ten thousand years,
Bright shining as the sun,
We've no less days to sing God's praise
Than when we first begun.

Conversely, it is true that after people have been in hell for ten thousand years, they have no fewer days to spend there, for eternity is always at the beginning. Oh, how kind God is to warn us by describing these end-time events now!

He said to me: 'It is done. I am the Alpha and the Omega, the Beginning and the End. To him who is thirsty I will give to drink without cost from the spring of the water of life' (Rev. 21:6).

Are you thirsty?

8

How to Handle Jealousy

Revelation 1:9

There are few people who have not been either the subject
or the object of jealousy at some time in their lives. Someone
has said that jealousy is the sin nobody talks about; I think it
is the sin nobody admits to – at least, readily. We do not like
admitting to being jealous because this exposes our insecurity
and weakness; the last thing we want another person to know
is that we are insecure. Yet the chances are, our jealousy is
one malady everybody else can see but us, and although we
cannot deny that there are also psychological implications,
fundamentally, jealousy is sin. Envy came into the world
because sin came into the world, and it was not long after
the fall of Adam and Eve that we see the first instance of
this sin. Cain and Abel were their sons, but one brother
became jealous of the other with tragic results:

> Now Abel kept flocks, and Cain worked the soil. In the course
> of time, Cain brought some of the fruits of the soil as an offering
> to the Lord. But Abel brought fat portions from some of the
> firstborn of his flock. The LORD looked with favour on Abel
> and his offering, but on Cain and his offering he did not look
> with favour. So Cain was very angry, and his face was
> downcast. . . . Now Cain said to his brother Abel, 'Let's go out
> to the field.' And while they were in the field, Cain attacked
> his brother Abel and killed him (Gen. 4:2–5, 8).

Cain's jealousy of Abel grew out of control, breaking the ties of brotherhood, and expressing itself in murder.

But if jealousy is not checked, it inevitably leads to greater sin, to a psychological disorder called 'paranoia', which is probably the most serious psychosis there is. When this happens, a person becomes increasingly suspicious of another and his imagination begins to run riot and eventually he suffers delusions of persecution. This psychosis can lead to murder. You may say, 'I know what it is to be jealous, but I would *never* commit murder.' But you do not *know* what you will do. Some of the worst crimes have been committed by the most unlikely people, who would not normally hurt a fly. So jealousy must be brought under control or it will result in your damnation – not just your damnation in this life but your eternal damnation. It is a most serious sin.

In Galatians 5 Paul described it among other 'acts of a sinful nature':

> The acts of the sinful nature are obvious: sexual immorality, impurity and debauchery; idolatry and witchcraft; hatred, discord, jealousy, fits of rage, selfish ambition, dissensions, factions and envy; drunkenness, orgies, and the like. I warn you, as I did before, that those who live like this will not inherit the kingdom of God (vv. 19–21).

We may define jealousy as an attitude of envy or resentment towards a more successful rival. Sometimes it results from frustrated attempts to achieve an ambition, and sometimes it results from seeing somebody has more talent, greater social advantages, more money, better looks or a better personality than we have. It may also arise when we see another succeeding where we have failed and we allow our resentment to grow into jealousy.

You will recall that I said earlier that it is not a sin we

easily detect in ourselves, but we can readily see it in others. For example, we can look at two people who are quarrelling, and if we are not involved we can see the contentious issue objectively and identify the cause as jealousy: it is so obvious to us. But we will not likely succeed in persuading the guilty party to admit this.

The reason it is easy to detect jealousy in others is they inevitably behave in a way that betrays their feelings. They are at odds with their environment: perhaps they are constantly agitated or nervous; they may be suspicious of others or stubborn. They express their envy by attacking the object of their resentment verbally and, sometimes, even by resorting to violence. Often they resort to public criticism; this has the effect of enhancing their own self-esteem and affords a bizarre kind of gratification.

However, we should recognize that some are more prone to jealousy than others. Even in the strongest of Christians, psychological weakness, retroactive to some childhood trauma perhaps, can cause feelings of envy to arise. An example of how this can happen is if parents favour one child above his siblings; jealousy of the other children in the family is the inevitable result. Often it is the firstborn in a family who is the most vulnerable, for when a new baby comes along, the oldest child is no longer the focus of attention. Another way parents can cause jealousy is by setting unrealistic goals for a child, who will struggle to reach these targets, casting an envious eye on other children who can cope easily.

Other insensitive adults who have an important role in a child's life may also be responsible for causing jealousy. This can happen at school, for example, when a teacher makes no secret of his dislike for a certain pupil, while openly favouring others in the class. The jealous feelings these actions arouse do not always disappear as the youngster grows older: they may remain, an undesirable emotional legacy of childhood.

However, being the object of jealousy is also problematic. Most of us know what it is to have somebody jealous of us. But I stress that we must be careful here, because it can lead to paranoia, which, as I said earlier, is a serious psychosis expressed in suspicion and delusions. Have you ever seen two people talking several yards away and thought, 'I know they are talking about *me*, because they are jealous of me'? We have all thought like that and it does not necessarily mean we are paranoid. But the fact that you think this way shows that the seed of this psychosis is there. It is also easy to try to explain unpopularity away by saying that the reason behind it is that others are simply jealous; you could be wrong. However, some of us project in this way more than others.

Yet what if another's jealousy of you is *real*? There could be many causes of this. Perhaps he or she envies your race, your social class, your wealth or your good looks. Moreover, if you are a Christian you should be aware that others may envy the spiritual gifts with which God has endowed you.

How do you handle a situation like this? The first thing to remember is not to take it personally. Come to see it as the other person's problem and pity him for he cannot help feeling this way. But remember, if you allow it to affect you then the problem becomes yours.

You need to identify the *real* enemy. It is a sign of spiritual maturity, when, like Paul, you can say, 'For our struggle is not against flesh and blood, but against the rulers, against the authorities, against the powers of this dark world and against the spiritual forces of evil in the heavenly realms' (Eph. 6:12). Paul identified the real enemy: the devil. So if you are the target of unjust criticism aimed to hurt you by attacking your character or by diminishing your influence, know that Satan is behind it all. However, you should also realize that you are no different, and in similar circumstances the chances are that you would react in the same way.

Earlier I said that it was difficult to detect jealousy in ourselves, so you may ask how you may recognize it and deal with it. So if you find yourself disliking somebody, ask yourself why. Is he more talented, more wealthy or more glamorous than you are? Does he have a better job or a higher position in society? Are you often critical of him? Then, when you recognize the cause of your attitude towards him is jealousy, examine yourself. Maybe you do not like to admit that you have any shortcomings, but a quick way to handle jealousy is to look at yourself realistically – this can be very sobering.

Have you come to accept yourself as you are? The problem is, most of us want to impute to ourselves certain talents that we do not, in fact, possess. For example, we may be envious of another person's job. Yet the truth may be that we could not manage to do it if we had it. Some years ago a book was published in America called *The Peter Principle*. Its theme was this: many people, because they are ambitious, are promoted to the level of their incompetence and find themselves at a level where they are unable to function, whereas at a lower level they had managed with ease. The author claimed this was true in all walks of life. So if you envy another person because of their job, ask yourself honestly whether you could do it and recognize your limitations.

However, we have a responsibility not only towards ourselves but to others.

First, a word to parents: I return to the point I raised earlier.

It is not easy for us as parents to understand the world in which our children live, but one of our tasks is to be sensitive to their feelings. So we should be careful not to set unrealistic goals before them that lead to frustration, for envy will result. We do our children no favour to set up rivalry among them. But, above all, we must *never* 'play favourites'; this can be so damaging.

Now a word to husbands and to wives: come to know your spouse's weakness. Do not aggravate your partner if he or she is jealous by nature. I know of many marriages that have broken down simply because one partner deliberately set out to make the other jealous. However, if your spouse's jealousy is pathological in nature, there is little you can do. This situation can be very serious and sad. But one of the best ways to cope in such a marriage is for the other partner to be very sensitive.

What about your relationship with those outside the immediate family circle? Do you like to have other people envy you? Do you do or say things that you know will make them jealous? For example, are you out to impress by name-dropping? Do you love to say things like, 'Well, as I was just saying to Her Majesty the Queen an hour ago...'? Do you brag about yourself, about your promotion or your income? If so, you need to change this behaviour, for you have a responsibility to others and so should avoid making them jealous of you.

What, then, is the connection between all that I have said so far and Revelation 1:9? Let us look at what it says:

I, John, your brother and companion in the suffering and kingdom and patient endurance that are ours in Jesus, was on the island of Patmos because of the word of God and the testimony of Jesus.

The man who said these words knew what it was to be both the subject and the object of jealousy.

We discover John was the subject of jealousy in Mark 10:35-45.

> Then James and John, the sons of Zebedee, came to him [Jesus].
> 'Teacher,' they said, 'we want you to do for us whatever we ask.'
>   'What do you want me to do for you?' he asked (vv. 35-36).

Note that Jesus didn't say, 'All right, I'll do it'; he asked what it was they wanted.

Sometimes our children will come up and beg, 'Will you do me a favour?' or 'Will you do something if I ask you?' James and John tried this childish ploy with Jesus: 'We want to ask something of you, and we want you to do it, *whatever* it is.' But Jesus said, 'Hold it! Tell me what it is first.' Then, blushing a little, they replied, 'Let one of us sit at your right and the other at your left in your glory.' John and his brother were plainly motivated by a spirit of jealousy, fearing that the other disciples would be exalted above them in heaven. But John also knew what it was to be the object of jealousy, as we see in John 21:18-22 where Jesus told Peter how he would die:

> 'I tell you the truth, when you were younger you dressed yourself and went where you wanted; but when you are old you will stretch out your hands, and someone else will dress you and lead you where you do not want to go.' Jesus said this to indicate the kind of death by which Peter would glorify God. Then he said to him, 'Follow me!'
>   Peter turned and saw that the disciple whom Jesus loved was following them. (This was the one who had leaned back against Jesus at the supper and had said, 'Lord, who is going

to betray you?') When Peter saw him, he asked, 'Lord, what about him?'

Jesus answered, 'If I want him to remain alive until I return, what is that to you? You must follow me.'

Clearly Peter was jealous of John.

So here in Revelation 1:9 we have a man who says, 'I am your brother.' The wonderful thing about the Bible is that the characters in its pages shared all our failings and weaknesses. I find this a great encouragement.

However, John, who identified himself with us in our weaknesses as our 'brother and companion', went on to show us the way to solve the problem of jealousy in ourselves. Let us look at the verse again:

> I, John, your brother and companion in the suffering and kingdom and patient endurance that are ours in Jesus, was on the island of Patmos because of the word of God and the testimony of Jesus.

The answer is, then, to recognize you are in a kingdom and patiently endure the trials that come your way. Let me explain further. John was speaking of a spiritual kingdom ruled by Jesus, and it is he, the King, who must receive all the honour and praise. God once said, 'I am the LORD; that is my name! I will not give my glory to another' (Isa. 42:8). We need to understand that Christ is King: we are his servants. But apart from this, there is no hierarchy in his kingdom; we are all co-heirs with him (Rom. 8:17). We are all equal: God loves us all the same. When we understand this, we will see that we have no cause to be jealous of anybody else. Greatness is a matter of doing God's will, and we receive our glory, not from others but from him. This is why the psalmist could say, 'I would rather be a door-keeper in the house of my God than dwell in the tents of the wicked' (Ps. 84:10).

Only God can deal with jealousy and only God can forgive it. But the Bible says, 'If we confess our sins, he is faithful and just and will forgive us our sins' (1 John 1:9). So confess your sin, receive God's pardon and take your place as a loyal subject in Jesus' kingdom.

9

How to Handle an Enemy

Revelation 1:9–10

Do you have an enemy? If your reply is 'No', then, do you realize how much of the Bible is irrelevant to you? After all, when we pray the Lord's Prayer, we say, 'Forgive us our trespasses, as we forgive those who trespass against us'. Christians certainly know what it is to have enemies. When they accept Jesus as their Saviour, they gain a new enemy: the devil. Not only that, they often find that the friends they had before become hostile towards them, and their loved ones often become their bitterest foes. Indeed, Paul said, 'In fact, everyone who wants to live a godly life in Christ Jesus will be persecuted' (2 Tim. 3:12).

John knew what it was like to face persecution. He had many enemies, who, after failing in their attempt to boil him in oil, had banished him to Patmos and left him there to die. But John had expected oppression, and he told us not to be surprised if the world hates us too (1 John 3:13).

We need look no further than the Bible to see how to cope with persecution, for the account of how David handled King Saul, who was his enemy, is instructive. The story of Saul's enmity towards David teaches us two things: (1) what our attitude toward an enemy should be, and (2) how to deal with that person.

However, I cannot go further without warning you again to be wary of projecting. We sometimes imagine we have an enemy when we do not, and this, as we saw in the previous chapter, borders on paranoia – the very essence of satanic oppression. Satan often attempts to inject us with a spirit of fear so we imagine the worst.

This is precisely what he did with Saul. Are you aware that whereas Saul was *truly* David's enemy, Saul only *thought* David was an enemy? This led to Saul seeking to take David's life, but the Bible tells us that David 'behaved himself wisely in all his ways' (1 Sam. 18:14, AV). Now what made the difference between David and Saul was that when the devil injected Saul with a spirit of fear, he began to imagine things; and the more David behaved himself wisely, the more it provoked Saul, until he was beside himself with suspicion and rage. So we must be cautious in thinking we have an enemy; this may not be the case.

Enemies come in degrees. At one end of the scale is the kind who simply try to provoke you or to annoy you, and, at the other, is the kind who wants to be rid of you entirely. So if you have an enemy, the first thing to do is to ask yourself how significant is the risk this person presents. Is he or she able to do you real harm? Some could not harm you because (1) they do not have the temperament to hurt you badly, or (2) they do not have sufficient power or the influence to do so; the most they can do is to upset you continually. If the latter is the case, the answer to your problem does not lie with your enemy but with you. This is because we are motivated by fear not love (2 Tim. 1:7; 1 John 4:18). What, then, about those who have real power to harm you? What if you have an enemy who wants to destroy you, maybe not physically, but, at least, to set you aside and bring you to nothing? We find the way to cope with a predicament like this by discovering how David dealt with Saul and then by looking at how John handled his situation on Patmos.

First, we see that David was an *innocent* victim of Saul's hostility. I say that because, if you have an enemy, you should ask yourself whether you have caused this situation to arise. Have you done or said anything to provoke this hostility? Has envy affected your attitude towards this person? Have you encouraged him or her to become jealous of *you*? (You may remember that I said in the previous chapter how you can deliberately set out to make others jealous.) If you have done that, you are largely responsible for the situation in which you now find yourself. Have you made an enemy through your own selfish ambition? Perhaps to get where you are now you have had to step on somebody else. This situation is not the same that faces you when you become a Christian, where people who appear to hate you really hate the Christ you serve: in these circumstances you are an innocent victim. However, if by your own attitudes and actions you are responsible for causing enmity in another, you are *not* blameless, and you need to recognize this.

But as I said, David, however, was the innocent victim of Saul's hostility. The evidence for this is that the Bible tells us that God was with David (1 Sam. 18:12, 14, 28). The writer of 1 Samuel took pains to stress this. Moreover, Saul realized that God had blessed David. The Bible reveals that David was gifted: he was a musician, a poet and a singer. (The Psalms are evidence of this.) He also had an uncanny ability to deal with wild beasts (1 Sam. 17:34-36), and we all know that he was an expert with a sling shot, for he felled Goliath with a stone from this weapon (1 Sam. 17:48-50). In fact, David was greatly talented, which Saul knew full well, and the consequence was that this, combined with David's popularity with the people, seemed a threat to Saul.

Now you must remember that if God has gifted you, this will endear you to some, but not to all. Do not make the mistake of thinking that because you have a particular talent or a particular ability that everybody will be proud of you. You will please some, but not all. Maybe you have a problem with somebody at work and he is jealous of your ability. If so, you must understand his problem and be careful not to hold it against him.

I said earlier that the Lord was with David. The result of God's presence with him was that he 'behaved himself wisely' (1 Sam. 18:5, 14, 15, 30, AV). None of David's skills and talents could help him deal with Saul; he needed wisdom beyond himself and grace that he did not possess by nature.

How, then, did God's presence enable David to behave so wisely with regard to Saul? We find the answer if we look at his story in the Bible.

First, we learn that he avoided a direct encounter with his enemy. In 1 Samuel 18 we read that David twice avoided being in Saul's presence:

> The next day an evil spirit from God came forcefully upon Saul. He was prophesying in his house, while David was playing the harp, as he usually did. Saul had a spear in his hand and he hurled it, saying to himself, 'I'll pin David to the wall.' But David eluded him twice (vv. 10-11).

This may surprise you. You may think that the wisest thing is always to have a direct encounter with your enemy. Yet that is not necessarily true, because if you have an enemy like David had, then you are dealing with an irrational person; you are dealing with a person driven by a spirit of fear, and a confrontation will only lead to an explosion of rage and could be disastrous.

The second thing we see is, in fact, the essence of David's wisdom: he regarded himself not as Saul's enemy but as

God's child. It is possible to be so preoccupied with your own problem, and to be so obsessed with your 'enemy', that you see yourself only as his opponent. What a poor self image! If, like David, you know you are a child of God, then you have God on your side and he has promised to vindicate you. I am not saying that vindication will come immediately or in the way you would like. Nevertheless, this is God's promise: 'It is mine to avenge; I will repay,' says the Lord (Rom. 12:19). This conviction lay behind everything that David did. He never tried to get even or to show himself to be more clever than Saul or to outmanoeuvre him. The certainty that underpinned David's wisdom was that vengeance belongs to the Lord. So David lived, not in fear, but knowing that God would take care of him.

Let us turn now to John to see how he behaved when his enemies banished him to Patmos for preaching the gospel? Remember he was the one who said, 'Do not be surprised, my brothers, if the world hates you' (1 John 3:13). How did he react? Did he feel bitter or sorry for himself? Was he preoccupied with his problem? No. He tells us, 'On the Lord's Day I was in the Spirit' (Rev. 1:10). He did not take that persecution personally: he knew that people hated him, not because of what he had done, but because of Christ who was in him.

One of the wonderful things about becoming a Christian is, like John, you can see what is behind the persecution you meet, and you do not take it personally but understand that it is God with whom others are angry: it is Christ they hate. John realized this and knew that he needed to be in God's presence, so he did not indulge in self-pity: he was 'in the Spirit'. It is possible to be so filled with the Spirit that you do not regard others as enemies, but you have a love for them.

An incident from the story of Corrie ten Boom demonstrates this is true. She was an extraordinary Dutch Christian lady. With her family she helped many Jews escape the Nazi persecution during the Second World War. Then, one day, the family was arrested and Corrie and her older sister Betsie were sent to a Nazi concentration camp. Sadly, Betsie did not survive the ill treatment she received.

Sometime after the war ended, Corrie returned to Germany to tell their story. When she was speaking at a church in Munich, she saw one of the guards who had mistreated them in Ravensbruch. As the church was emptying after the meeting, he went to see her, claiming he had become a Christian and offered her his hand. But at first anger and bitterness filled her and she thought, 'What shall I do? How *can* I shake his hand? No. The way I feel can't be right. Surely God can forgive this person who hurt my sister!' Then she began to pray that God would fill her with love for this man. As she took his outstretched hand, she experienced a love for him that almost overwhelmed her, and Corrie found she could forgive after all. Corrie ten Boom was a Spirit-filled Christian.

Do you know what the fruit of the Spirit is? Paul tells us in Galatians 5:22-23: 'The fruit of the Spirit is love, joy, peace, patience, kindness, goodness, faithfulness, gentleness and self-control.' When we have the Holy Spirit, we grow the fruit of that Spirit, the fruit of love. When we become Christians, God shares himself with us and we begin to radiate his beauty. This is not because we are better than others: we remain human and we are often tempted to do wrong. The difference is that God has promised to be with us so we can overcome these problems.

Sometimes it happens that a Christian feels he has an enemy who is a fellow Christian. But a fellow Christian is *not* an enemy but a brother or a sister in Christ, and God loves him or her as much as he loves you. You may *think* that God loves you more but this is not so. This is why I pointed out in the previous chapter that there is no room for jealousy in Christ's kingdom. 'I John [am] your brother' (Rev. 1:9). We are brothers, we are sisters 'in the suffering and kingdom and patient endurance that are ours in Jesus ...' (v. 9).

But if a fellow Christian shows hostility towards you, what are you to do? The answer is to remember that what you want above all is the truth; you do not want necessarily to be proved right. If you find the truth, there is always the possibility that the other person is right, not you. As a Christian, you must always bear that in mind.

Yet suppose you are a Christian and your enemy is not, what then? In this situation you must remember that the other person is not *able* to forgive: he has no grace to do it. Above all, you should bear in mind that he or she is motivated by a spirit of fear. Remember what Paul said to Timothy: 'God hath not given us the spirit of fear; but of power, and of love, and of a sound mind' (2 Tim. 1:7, AV). But your enemy does not have that. Consider his plight: his downfall is inevitable, but it is not *your* job to bring it about.

If you are not a Christian, I must tell you that you cannot handle your enemy until you have God with you. Furthermore, you should know that you have enemies you have not considered before: perhaps you have been laying the blame at the feet of the wrong person. Begin with yourself: you are your own enemy, for you are living for yourself. Paul warned of the consequences of this:

Do not be deceived: God cannot be mocked. A man reaps what he sows. The one who sows to please his sinful nature, from that nature will reap destruction; the one who sows to please the Spirit, from the Spirit will reap eternal life (Gal. 6:7–8).

So if you are living for yourself, although you may go through life blaming everybody else for your problems, you are your own enemy.

But you have another enemy, one who can be surprisingly self-effacing: the devil. Satan works against you to try to ensure you do not become a Christian. Not only are you in transgressions and sins (Eph. 2:1), but Satan has blinded you to your spiritual condition. Paul said, 'The god of this age has blinded the minds of unbelievers, so that they cannot see the light of the gospel' (2 Cor. 4:4). Moreover, Satan stays in the background working to maintain your spiritual blindness.

However, the worst enemy of all that you can ever have is God himself. If you are not a Christian, he is angry with you and you are his natural enemy, for you love 'darkness instead of light' (John 3:19). God has given you his Law and you have rejected it; he has sent his Son into the world but you have gone on your way. Jesus said, 'Whoever believes in him [God's Son] is not condemned, but whoever does not believe stands condemned already because he has not believed in the name of God's one and only Son' (John 3:18). Remember one day God will send his enemies to hell. I beg you to be reconciled with him. Jesus, who forgave those who nailed him to the cross (Luke 23:34), offers you forgiveness now, and when you accept his pardon, you will see that if God forgives you, then you can forgive others.

10

How to Handle Death

Revelation 1:9–11

We cannot pass over the subject of death when we remember that John, on the isle of Patmos, was waiting to die. Yet he could face death without fear and say, 'On the Lord's Day I was in the Spirit . . .' (Rev. 1:10).

Death is the most obvious fact of life, yet it probably causes more secret concern than any other theological subject. I say 'secret concern' because death is something that people do not often talk about, but the worst thing we can do is to repress this subject. Let me explain. Repression is a defence mechanism. We often suppress what the conscious mind finds too painful by denying it exists; we push it down into the subconscious and it lies there, but it will continue to affect us by causing illness, headaches, high blood pressure and insomnia, for example. God created us in such a way that repressing traumatic events or failing to face up to unpleasant facts is never successful, and when we confront our anxiety about death we will be surprised how much our general, psychological and physical condition will improve.

Note I call it a 'theological' subject. Obviously death is not a topic limited to theology; nevertheless, theology alone has the answer to our concern. Indeed death is a subject at the heart of all sound theology. The wonderful thing is, the message is one of hope, because theology teaches that physical death is not the end. In fact, the Bible talks about the *death* of death (1 Cor. 15:26; Rev. 20:14; 21:4). So if you want to know how to handle death, you ought to know what God's word says about it.

I believe it gives us seven elementary lessons.

The first lesson the Bible teaches is that death is the punishment for sin. The Bible tells us that God did not intend that men and women rebel against him. In Genesis 2 we read:

> The LORD God took the man and put him in the Garden of Eden to work it and take care of it. And the LORD God commanded the man, 'You are free to eat from any tree in the garden; but you must not eat from the tree of the knowledge of good and evil, for when you eat of it you will surely die' (vv. 15-17).

Death came into being only as the result of sin. If people had not sinned they would have lived in their natural state for ever. We have little idea what life would have been like, but what we do know is that when God created the world it was perfect: he created Adam and Eve perfect beings in his own image and likeness (Gen. 1:27). But once they sinned, things were never the same again, and death came into the world. Paul put it this way: '...sin entered the world through one man, and death through sin, and in this way death came to all men, because all sinned' (Rom. 5:12). Then, in Romans 6:23, he added, 'The wages of sin is death.'

Because God created us in his own likeness it means we have a conscience: this is what separates us from all other forms of life. God's image is stamped upon the human race, but when Adam and Eve sinned that image was almost effaced. Nevertheless, a vestige remains in the form of our conscience, so, according to Paul, people are without excuse if they turn from the knowledge of God, for he is knowable through nature and through conscience (Rom. 1:20).

The second important lesson is that death is not the end. Because God created us in his image, he gave us souls that are immortal. Now many contemporary theologians believe that the notion that we have immortal souls was simply borrowed from Greek Platonism. In fact it is also an implicit Hebrew concept. We see proof of this in 1 Kings 17:17-24, where we read how Elijah prayed over the dead son of the widow at Zarephath. He stretched himself out on the child three times and pleaded with God, crying, '"O LORD my God, let this boy's life (soul) return to him!" The LORD heard Elijah's cry, and the boy's life returned to him.' So the immortality of the human soul is not exclusively a Greek idea: it is biblical. Jesus himself said that humans are immortal. He once asked, 'What good will it be for a man if he gains the whole world, yet forfeits his soul?' (Matt. 16:26).

The third lesson the Bible teaches about death is that God himself became man to deliver you and me from its clutches. This is the most extraordinary thing of all. And the more you come to know God, the more amazed you become that he sent Jesus, who, as we have seen, is fully God, into the world to become man. Do you know that God did not *have* to do that? God could have let creation continue in its fallen state and just send everybody to hell when they die. Now you may stay awake at night asking, 'How could God send anybody to a place of eternal torment?' But the question you really need to ask is, 'How could God send his Son into a world that hates him?'

This event was so extraordinary and so significant that John began his Gospel by speaking of this:

> In the beginning was the Word [Jesus], and the Word was with God, and the Word was God. He was with God in the beginning.
>
> Through him all things were made; without him nothing was made that has been made. . . . The Word became flesh and made his dwelling among us (John 1:1–3, 14).

To think that God became man is amazing! But that is not all. The writer to the Hebrews tells us this:

> [Jesus] was made a little lower than the angels, [and is] now crowned with glory and honour because he suffered death, so that by the grace of God he might taste death for everyone (Heb. 2:9).

So not only did God become man, but as a man he died for us all! However, there is more to see, for in the same chapter we read:

> Since the children [of God] have flesh and blood, he too shared in their humanity so that by his death he might destroy him who holds the power of death—that is, the devil—and free those who all their lives were held in slavery by their fear of death (vv. 14–15).

Here we find what perhaps is one of the most stupendous claims about Jesus: he came to deliver us from the fear of death. So the fact that if you are not already a Christian you are afraid to die is nothing new; the Bible acknowledges that people fear death. However, as we have just seen, it also claims we may be delivered from this fear, and to this end God himself became man and died for us. It is amazing! Charles Wesley put it like this:

Amazing love!
How can it be
That thou, my God, shouldst die for me?

The fourth lesson we learn from Scripture is that Jesus, the God-man, rose from the dead so that we too may one day have a resurrection. All four Gospels record the fact that Jesus rose from the dead on that first Easter day (Matt. 28; Mark 16; Luke 24; John 20). However, Jesus did not rise from the grave only on his own account but so that we who would have died the eternal death, which is the penalty for sin, also might live. Paul knew that Jesus' resurrection was essential to our future hope. He put it this way:

> If the dead are not raised, then Christ has not been raised either. And if Christ has not been raised, your faith is futile; you are still in your sins. Then those also who have fallen asleep in Christ are lost (1 Cor. 15:16-18).

He continued his theme saying, 'If only for this life we have hope in Christ, we are to be pitied more than all men' (v.19). This contradicts the popular, sentimental notion that Christianity is the best way of life, even if there is no life to come. According to Paul this is nonsense. Christianity is *not* a way of life in the first place: it is a cross we bear – a stigma! Why do we keep going? Because we are looking for a city beyond.

The fifth lesson to learn is that Jesus offers eternal life to *everybody*. John 3:16 makes this crystal clear: 'For God so loved the world that he gave his one and only Son, that *whoever* [my italics] believes in him shall not perish but have eternal life.' Jesus offers eternal life to all men and women without exception. Hebrews 2:9 confirms this: 'Jesus . . . suffered death, so that by the grace of God he might taste death for everyone.'

The sixth lesson is this: receiving Christ does not exempt us from the first death (physical death); nobody can avoid this for we are all sinners (Rom. 3:23) and 'the wages of sin is death' (Rom. 6:23). But nobody has to fear the first death; we will all survive it, because, as we have seen, when Jesus returns all the dead will be resurrected to face judgment (Rev. 20:12-13). However, becoming a Christian does exempt us from the second death. You may remember Jesus' great promise to the church at Smyrna: 'He who overcomes will not be hurt at all by the second death' (Rev. 2:11).

And this leads me to the seventh lesson: the second death is an *eternal* death because man is made in God's image. You might say that the essence of God is that he is eternal. (I use this expression cautiously because it is impossible to sum up God phenomenologically; we cannot tie him up in a box, as it were, and say, 'This is God.') And when he chose to make the human race in his own likeness, he gave it the quality of eternality. So the eternal death is an eternal dying. This is why John described hell as a lake of fire that burns for ever (Rev. 20:10). One day we will all stand before our Maker to be judged, and on that day some will go to this place of eternal punishment. Revelation 20:12-15 describes the Final Judgment like this:

> I saw the dead, great and small, standing before the throne, and books were opened. Another book was opened, which is the book of life. The dead were judged according to what they had done as recorded in the books. The sea gave up the dead that were in it, and death and Hades gave up the dead that were in them, and each person was judged according to what he had done. Then death and Hades were thrown into the lake of fire. The lake of fire is the second death. If anyone's name was not found written in the book of life, he was thrown into the lake of fire.

Now for an animal, physical death is final. But we are created in God's image, and for that reason he who is eternal will consign those who are not his to eternal punishment.

These are the elementary lessons the Bible teaches about death. However, I want us now to consider two things we may learn from the story of how Jesus raised Lazarus from the dead (John 11).

The first is Jesus' own attitude toward death. This has much to teach us.

Lazarus and Jesus were friends, and when Lazarus became gravely ill his sisters, Mary and Martha, sent Jesus a message to tell him their brother was ill. They knew that Jesus would come and that he had power to heal their brother for they had watched him perform so many miracles. But Jesus' reaction to the news of his friend's illness at first seems hard to understand. He said, 'This sickness will not end in death. No, it is for God's glory so that God's Son may be glorified through it' (v. 4).

This seems a strange comment, coming from someone who was a close friend. Yet did you know that is the Christian attitude toward any sickness? Indeed, I will go a step further and say the Christian is one who looks at everything in life as ultimately redounding to God's glory.

The second thing we learn is that Jesus was in no hurry to get to Lazarus. Now this may seem even more strange to you. Verse 6 says, 'When he heard that Lazarus was sick, he stayed where he was two more days.' What kind of friendship is that? But Christians learn that if God delays his answer to prayer, it is with good reason. We do not always get an answer when we want it.

His disciples must have been puzzled by this delay and when Jesus told them, 'Lazarus is dead' (v.14), they must have wondered why he had allowed this to happen to his friend. People today often ask why God allows tragedies to happen. Indeed you may be one who says, 'I will become a Christian when I know *why* God allows these things.' No. You would not. The very fact you say that is the proof that you would *not* be converted. Moreover, God would do you no favour to answer that question.

Let me explain. One of the most interesting verses in the whole of the New Testament is John 11:15. After telling his disciples Lazarus had died, Jesus said, 'For your sake I am glad I was not there.' This is an amazing statement. Why did Jesus say this? The reason becomes clear in the second half of the verse: ' . . . so that you may believe'. You see, if Jesus had been there and healed Lazarus immediately, there would have been no opportunity for anybody to exercise *faith*. So the fact that you do not receive the answers to such questions as 'Why does God allow bad things to happen?' and 'Why is there so much suffering and evil in the world?' is a blessing, for it gives you an opportunity to believe, because it is only when you have faith in Jesus that you can be saved.

But what was the attitude of Mary and Martha?

Well, theirs was a very carnal attitude. Martha began to scold Jesus when he arrived: 'Lord, if you had been here, my brother would not have died' (v. 21). So we see that Martha blamed Jesus for her brother's death. Later, Mary said the same thing and others joined in the criticism too, saying, 'Could not he who opened the eyes of the blind man have kept this man from dying?' (v. 37). This is the way unconverted people always think. They say, 'If God is all-powerful, why did he allow sin to come into the world? Why do we see so many tragic things happening?'

Jesus' response to Martha and Mary in the face of their anger was amazing. He did not rebuke them: the Bible tells us that he wept (v. 35). So if you want to know how God reacts to your questions, the answer is, he weeps. But he will not give you the answer you seek, because then faith would be impossible and you would have no hope of eternal life. Yet in withholding the answer from you, he weeps.

What, then, should be *our* attitude towards death? First, we should remember that grieving when we lose somebody we love is right. We can also weep with others when they suffer loss. Jesus identified with the mourners in their distress and wept with them, so we may weep too. In fact, weeping in the face of death is a healthy response, for it shows you are facing reality. I have been a minister for many years and have preached at many funerals. I have had to console many people, but I am concerned most about those who cannot cry. Admittedly, sometimes it is because of their temperament, but usually it is because they are not facing up to what has happened. They say, 'I can't believe it.' For weeks they are in a state of denial: they will not accept their loss and so are unable to cry. However, the right way to handle death is to bring it into the open: do not deny it. Remember you may weep. If Jesus could weep in the face of death, then it is all right for you to cry too.

You may ask, 'What about my loved ones who are not Christians when they die?' There is only one answer to that: you must surrender them to the God who made them. Nobody can take the place of another or answer for them. Even those who are closest to us cannot take our place at the Judgment. God created us as individuals and as individuals we must answer to him. In any case, we do not know where those people are who – in our opinion – were not saved. Who can say for sure that such a person did not call upon the name of the Lord?

How, then, should you handle the prospect of your own

death? My answer is, act now: do not wait until it is too late. It is so simple. Acknowledge before God that you are a sinner; thank him for sending his Son into the world to taste death for you (Heb. 2:9), and receive him as your Saviour. You may then face death without fear, for you will have eternal life.

11

How to Face the Unexpected

Revelation 1:9–10

Fear of what the future holds in store begins in childhood: we discover that our parents and friends may disappoint us or even reject us; we learn that illness or accident may happen suddenly and that people we love die; we learn that we do not always succeed and begin to fear failure. 'Will my grades be high enough in my school report to please mum and dad? Will I pass my exams and get a good job when I leave school?' We can all remember anxiously asking ourselves these kinds of questions.

Yet wondering what the future holds in store does not end with our childhood. As adults, we know that life is filled with uncertainty and that even within the short span of twenty-four hours something can happen that will change our lives for ever. Furthermore, none of us knows when death will call us to stand before our Maker and account for the way we have lived.

I think we can define maturity as 'learning to face the unexpected'. Now if ever a person had to face the unexpected, it was John. So we will find it instructive to see how he faced his uncertain and unpromising future on the island of Patmos.

When John was sent into exile, he was an old man, probably about ninety years old at the time. He had outlived all the other disciples, who, as far as we know, were all martyred by the time John was sent into exile. According to tradition, John's enemies had previously tried to kill him too by boiling him to death in oil. Apparently they lit the fire under the pot of oil and thrust him in, but strangely, nothing happened: he refused to die. This made them afraid to try again, so they decided the only sure way to be rid of him was to banish him to a remote location and leave him to die.

How was he able to cope? John knew that faith was important. Earlier, in his Gospel, he had recorded these words of Jesus: 'In this world you will have trouble. But take heart! I have overcome the world' (John 16:33). John knew that victory is certain for anybody who believes in Jesus, and in his first letter to the church he said, 'Everyone born of God overcomes the world. This is the victory that has overcome the world, even our faith' (1 John 5:4). This gives you an idea of how John felt and how much he trusted in the Lord.

It is one thing to believe something theoretically, but quite another to put faith into practice. When trouble comes, many Christians *say* they believe the Bible but when they have problems and when tragedy comes into their lives they go to pieces. They need to take firm hold of what John had grasped, 'Everyone born of God overcomes the world. This is the victory that overcomes the world, even our faith.'

Now, John put his faith into practice. Verse 10 shows us how he did this: it says, 'On the Lord's Day I was in the Spirit . . .'. That was how John faced the unexpected.

The psalmist once said:

He that dwelleth in the secret place of the most High
shall abide under the shadow of the Almighty (Ps. 91:1, AV).

Although it may not be immediately obvious, there is a

connection between these words and the words of John when he said, 'I was in the Spirit on the Lord's Day.' The psalmist's message was of the security that a close relationship with the Lord brings through the indwelling Spirit. John also experienced such assurance, for he too was 'in the Spirit'.

You will note, however, that Psalm 91 refers to the '*secret* place'. We need to understand the Holy Spirit is secret: he is hidden. Failure to grasp this will cause confusion.

Unlike the Holy Spirit, Jesus is not secret: he is not hidden. Thousands of people saw him during his lifetime on earth. They watched him teach and witnessed the many wonderful miracles he performed, and they saw him nailed to the cross. The things Jesus did were plain for all to see: his life was an open book. Yet whereas Jesus' life was lived in full public view, the Holy Spirit is self-effacing. This is what I mean by 'secret'. The Holy Spirit seldom calls attention to himself. We cannot see him or touch him, and in that sense we could say that we cannot empirically know him.

We are not to exalt the Holy Spirit. His function is to promote the glory of *Jesus* and make him known (John 16:14). To put it another way, the Spirit makes Christ as real in our hearts as Jesus had been to the disciples who saw him. The Spirit himself, however, is hidden: he points men and women to Jesus.

So John was 'in the Spirit', and, like the psalmist, he could say, 'He that dwelleth in the secret place of the most High shall abide under the shadow of the Almighty.'

Another strategy John used in coping with the unexpected was to pray. Alone and thus without Christian fellowship, he turned to God. Remember, if you are lonely you too can pray. Sometimes, when all else fails, God allows bad things to happen to us to bring us to the place of prayer.

However, we must recognize that John's prayer was no

ordinary prayer: he was 'in the Spirit'. How does one get 'in the Spirit?' The question is important, because until you know what it is like to be in the Spirit, you will never know how to face the unexpected. Yet *you* cannot initiate this. The Holy Spirit cannot be manipulated by your hands or by your will. I have heard it said that people can 'work up' the Spirit. This is utterly false. The Spirit must come to you first.

Next you should know that to abide in 'the secret place of the most High', is to accept what the Spirit reveals: Jesus Christ, the Son of God, came to the world, and when he was crucified, more was happening than was visible to the human eye, for on the cross God punished his perfectly righteous Son. You may think God was cruel and very unfair to punish Jesus, who knew no sin. Nevertheless, I want you to know that is how much God loves you. He sent his Son into the world and punished him instead of you, and he laid all your sins on him.

You may ask, 'Am I guilty?' The answer is, if you have ever committed *one* sin, you are guilty. Furthermore, sin must be punished. 'But why can't I atone for my own sins?' you may reply. 'I will show God I'm serious by going without a treat or fasting for a while. Then, if I try to do better in future, won't that impress him?' But the answer is 'No'. You are not dealing with the God of your imagination: a jolly St Nicholas in the sky, whose only aim is to indulge you; you are dealing with the Most High God, who will not leave the guilty unpunished (Exod. 34:7). You will never satisfy God's justice until you accept what his word says, and what the Holy Spirit reveals, is true: Jesus, God's own Son, paid your penalty for your sin. The only thing God demands from you is that you believe his word; this is the only way people are ever converted.

Your next question may be, 'If I accept what is revealed, how will this help me face the unknown?' We find the answer when we return to Psalm 91:

> Surely he shall deliver thee from the snare of the fowler,
> and from the noisome pestilence.
> He shall cover thee with his feathers,
> and under his wings shalt thou trust:
> his truth shall be thy shield and buckler.
> Thou shalt not be afraid for the terror by night;
> nor for the arrow that flieth by day;
> nor for the pestilence that walketh in darkness (vv. 3–6, AV).

So the first thing we see is that God will give you deliverance from the *fear* of the unexpected.

The second thing to see is that if you accept what is open and revealed, God will give you special protection. Look at verse 7:

> A thousand shall fall at thy side,
> And ten thousand at thy right hand;
> But it shall not come nigh thee (AV).

God has a way of protecting his own with singular mercy. Do you know why? It is because when you accept his Son, who bought you with his own blood, you become a part of God's family: you become his child. 1 John 3:1 says, 'How great is the love the Father has lavished on us, that we should be called children of God! And that is what we are.' So now the things that concern you, concern him; your problems become his problems and your cares become his cares. He enters into a covenant with you, and *everything* that happens to you will be with his divine permission. When you become a Christian, you may face the future without fear.

John could face the unexpected because he was 'in the Spirit'. You may ask, 'When will the Spirit of the Lord come on me?' The answer is simple: the Holy Spirit has *already* come, because Jesus said, 'The words I have spoken to you are spirit and they are life' (John 6:63). He has come in God's word with the best news that you will ever hear: God has taken on your case and invites you to receive Jesus as your Saviour. The Bible tells us, 'Everyone who trusts in him will never be put to shame' (Rom. 10:11), and if you come to see it, then you are like John, who said, 'On the Lord's Day I was in the Spirit . . . '

12

The Voice from Behind

Revelation 1:10–20

In Revelation 1:10 John begins to tell us what happened to him after he was exiled to the Isle of Patmos. He said, 'On the Lord's Day I was in the Spirit, and I heard behind me a loud voice like a trumpet.' Then he states three things regarding his experience. First, John describes his state of mind; second, he tells us when the experience happened; and third, he tells us what happened to him.

He said, 'I was in the Spirit'. In other words, he had no sense of worry or anxiety, for the Holy Spirit brings peace and relieves the cares that otherwise almost overwhelm us. The safest place to be is in the Spirit. This, then, was John's state of mind when he was banished to the island of Patmos. He was not upset about his exile, nor did he panic; we find him 'in the Spirit'.

The Bible tells us that he was 'in the Spirit on the Lord's Day'. Now some believe that we should interpret this as 'the day of the Lord', meaning that John really meant that there was a sort of translation from the present moment to the eschatological day of the Lord. I suppose one could make a case supporting that view, but I tend to believe that what was really happening on this day was that John was carried into the Spirit in a timeless way, and 'the Lord's Day' simply means the particular day that the Holy Spirit chose to come to John.

But it may have been an intentional ambiguity, referring to the content of the vision he was going to describe as well as the day God chose to give it.

I think this happened on a Sunday, for we know that in the early Christian tradition the expression, 'the Lord's Day', increasingly referred to the first day of the week. It was a time when Christians met to commemorate the resurrection and began to meet to have the Lord's Supper. So probably this is what John meant, and knowing what day it was, and being unable to have fellowship with other Christians, he did the next best thing: he worshipped and prayed alone.

But something happened that he had not counted on. He said, 'I was in the Spirit, and I heard behind me a loud voice like a trumpet' (v. 10). It is this voice that came from behind him that we are to consider in this chapter. John did not imagine this voice; it was from an external source; it was a voice beyond the natural realm – a voice that was *super*natural.

Nowadays there is much interest in the supernatural, and many, seeking some kind of guidance about their future, turn to astrology. Millions of Britons and Americans now take their astrological charts very seriously, which, of course, are utter nonsense. But also dangerous; it is of Satan. Is it not strange that modern men and women no longer believe in what they read in the Bible, in such things as the Genesis account of creation, heaven and hell, and the Second Coming, and yet they are concerned about something as unscientific as astrology!

Another thing we know about this voice is that it was unexpected. John was 'in the Spirit' on the Lord's Day; he was praying; he was doing the only thing possible. He expected to die, for as far as we know, Patmos was uninhabited and there were no people for John to talk to and nobody to bring him food. He was alone, and there was nothing to do but to pray. Sometimes God will bring us to such a state. President Abraham Lincoln once said, 'I am constrained to go to my knees when I know there is no place else to go.' Now, for John, praying was a happy activity, because he had learned to have fellowship with God. He said in 1 John 1:3, 'Our fellowship is with the Father and with his Son, Jesus Christ.' John was praying, and the voice took him by surprise.

It was a voice from behind him, and it was so real that John said, 'I turned around to see the voice that was speaking to me' (Rev. 1:12). He tried to give us a hint of what it sounded like, and the best description he could find was that it was 'a voice like a trumpet'. Hearing God speak like that must be wonderful!

In Exodus 19 we have a description of God's voice, not unlike the voice John heard.

> On the morning of the third day there was thunder and lightning, with a thick cloud over the mountain, and a very loud trumpet blast. Everyone in the camp trembled. Then Moses led the people out of the camp to meet with God, and they stood at the foot of the mountain. Mount Sinai was covered with smoke, because the Lord descended on it in fire. The smoke billowed up from it like smoke from a furnace, the whole mountain trembled violently, and the sound of the trumpet grew louder and louder. Then Moses spoke and the voice of God answered him (vv. 16–19).

God was about to give Moses the Ten Commandments because people then were living very wickedly, and they had betrayed the promise to the patriarchs, Abraham, Isaac and Jacob. Things had come to such a pass that God stepped in and gave them moral laws. God did not *have* to do it. He could have destroyed them all. The same is true for you: God does not *have* to speak to you. Perhaps you are in trouble and you have ignored your conscience and continued in your rebellious way. God does not have to say anything further to you. In Moses' time God was angry with those who rebelled against his promise and were behaving in such a way that they brought disgrace and dishonour upon his holy name. So God spoke and the people trembled. As the psalmist said, 'He lifts his voice, the earth melts' (Ps. 46:6).

God once asked Job, 'Can your voice thunder like his?' (Job 40:9). But nobody can speak like God speaks. His voice is more powerful than all the forces of the universe combined. His voice brought creation into existence. 'In the beginning God created the heavens and the earth . . . And God said, "Let there be light"' (Gen. 1:1, 3). I want you to know that God could do to you whatever he wanted, simply by using his voice. It is so powerful that he can speak in your life and so straighten it out in a way you have never been able to do. He can come to where you are, turn you around and set you on a right path.

Do you know it was God's voice that authenticated his Son? When Jesus was baptized and was coming out of the water, a voice from heaven said, 'This is my Son, whom I love; with him I am well pleased' (Matt. 3:17). God put his seal on his Son openly by his voice from heaven. He not only did it openly, but he did it again secretly with Peter, James and John when they went up with Jesus to a high mountain and Jesus was transfigured before them. Then that voice came again, 'This is my Son, whom I love; with him I am well pleased' (Matt. 17:5).

God said he was well pleased with his Son and those words should be some of the happiest words you ever hear. I will tell you why. He is certainly not pleased with you if you are not a Christian, for your ways are contrary to his ways. God is holy; God is righteous and just. Because he is just, he must punish sin, and because you are a sinner, he must punish you. Exodus 34:7 tells us, 'He does not leave the guilty unpunished.' You are guilty in his eyes. But *you* can do nothing to remove your guilt, because your best intentions still fall short of the standard he demands. For example, your best intentions will always be selfish; your most ideal motives will still have a vestige of self-interest. But as long as you are self-centred you cannot please him. God is a God of glory. He said, 'I am the Lord; that is my name! I will not give my glory to another' (Isa. 42:8). But the voice from heaven said, 'This is my Son, whom I love; with him I am well pleased' (Matt. 17:5). Jesus pleased God and because he did there is hope for you.

It was Jesus' voice that struck down Saul of Tarsus on the road to Damascus, stopping him in his tracks. A brilliant light flashed around Saul and a voice said, 'Saul, Saul, why do you persecute me?' (Acts 9:4). Saul could do nothing but cry out, 'Who are you, Lord?' (v. 5).

However, I must also say this: someday God's people will hear Jesus' voice. The apostle Paul describes that day like this:

> Listen, I tell you a mystery: We will not all sleep, but we will all be changed—in a flash, in the twinkling of an eye, at the last trumpet. For the trumpet will sound, the dead will be raised imperishable, and we will be changed. For the perishable must clothe itself with the imperishable, and the mortal with immortality. When the perishable has been clothed with the imperishable, and the mortal with immortality, then the saying that is written will come true: 'Death has been swallowed up in victory' (1 Cor. 15:51–54).

In 1 Thessalonians 4:13–18 Paul had this to say about the coming of the Lord:

Brothers, we do not want you to be ignorant about those who fall asleep, or to grieve like the rest of men, who have no hope. We believe that Jesus died and rose again and so we believe that God will bring with Jesus those who have fallen asleep in him. According to the Lord's own word, we tell you that we who are still alive, who are left till the coming of the Lord, will certainly not precede those who have fallen asleep. For the Lord himself will come down from heaven, with a loud command, with the voice of the archangel and with the trumpet call of God, and the dead in Christ will rise first. After that, we who are still alive and are left will be caught up together with them in the clouds to meet the Lord in the air. And so we will be with the Lord forever. Therefore, encourage each other with these words.

A day when the voice like a trumpet will sound again! I have a secret ambition to hear that voice in my lifetime. I love to think that God will cause the sound of the trumpet to be heard around the globe and that this awful world will be brought to an end. Then every knee will bow before King Jesus (Rom. 14:11).

Finally, I must tell you that Jesus' voice is a voice that will someday pronounce the eternal doom of unbelievers when the Son of Man comes in his glory, an event that happens at the same time as that trumpet blast. Matthew 25:41–46 says this:

Then he will say . . . 'Depart from me, you who are cursed, into the eternal fire prepared for the devil and his angels. For I was hungry and you gave me nothing to eat, I was thirsty and you gave me nothing to drink, I was a stranger and you did not invite me in, I needed clothes and you did not clothe me, I was sick and in prison and you did not look after me.'

They also will answer, 'Lord, when did we see you hungry or thirsty or a stranger or needing clothes or sick or in prison, and did not help you?'

He will reply, 'I tell you the truth, whatever you did not do for one of the least of these, you did not do for me.'

Then they will go away to eternal punishment, but the righteous to eternal life.

The book of Revelation also describes the voice in another way:

A third angel followed them and said in a loud voice: 'If anyone worships the beast and his image and receives his mark on the forehead or on the hand, he, too, will drink of the wine of God's fury, which has been poured full strength into the cup of his wrath. He will be tormented with burning sulphur in the presence of the holy angels and of the Lamb. And the smoke of their torment rises for ever and ever. There is no rest day or night for those who worship the beast and his image. . .' (Rev. 14:9–11).

This is God's word: the voice of Jesus will sound and declare your doom.

Have you heard that voice? A voice stopping you in your tracks; a voice that makes you turn and see your life as it really is, a voice that does not *have* to speak to you any more than it had to speak to that wicked generation bringing dishonour upon God's name. That voice speaks to you now. 'Come now, let us reason together,' says the Lord. 'Though your sins are like scarlet, they shall be as white as snow; though they are red as crimson, they shall be like wool' (Isa. 1:18). The voice you hear now is one of forgiveness. Listen while there is still time.

13

Finding Jesus

Revelation 1:10–20

Who is Jesus? This question arouses great interest and has prompted much discussion throughout history. To decide what we mean by the person of Jesus Christ, in the following chapters we will look at John's description of Jesus in Revelation 1.

On the Lord's Day John was 'in the Spirit' when he heard from behind him a voice like a trumpet saying:

> Write on a scroll what you see and send it to the seven churches: to Ephesus, Smyrna, Pergamum, Thyatira, Sardis, Philadelphia and Laodicea. I turned around to see the voice that was speaking to me. And when I turned I saw seven golden lampstands, and among the lampstands was someone 'like a son of man' (vv. 11–13).

Then comes that marvellous, extraordinary description of Jesus in verses 13 to 16.

> [He was] dressed in a robe reaching down to his feet and with a golden sash around his chest. His head and hair were white like wool, as white as snow, and his eyes were like blazing fire. His feet were like bronze glowing in a furnace, and his voice was like the sound of rushing waters. In his right hand he held seven stars, and out of his mouth came a sharp double-edged sword. His face was like the sun shining in all its brilliance.

I think there are three things we should bear in mind when we consider this description of Jesus.

First, we are dealing with a *vision*. I stress that it is a vision, because John tells us that in the midst of the seven lampstands was 'someone like a son of man'. John did not see him directly, for the Son of Man himself was at the right hand of God; Jesus did not leave the throne and go to Patmos and actually manifest himself.

Not only is Jesus at the right hand of God, but he does not look like the figure in the vision. If God permitted us to see Jesus as he is at this very moment, he would look as he did to the disciples after his resurrection. They saw the same person that they had known for the previous three years. Though his body is glorified and transformed, it is the same Jesus. This same Jesus ascended to heaven, and if we were to see him now that is the way he would look.

The Bible says, 'There is one God and one mediator between God and men, the man Christ Jesus' (1 Tim. 2:5). I think one of the most important things that you can understand is that Jesus is the one seated in heaven at God's right hand; he is the God-man, the Word made flesh. But do not underestimate this fact: he is a *man*. If we saw him now, he would look like a man. Jesus is in heaven interceding for us.

Moreover, we read in Hebrews 4:15, 'We do not have a high priest who is unable to sympathise with our weaknesses, but we have one who has been tempted in every way, just as we are—yet was without sin.' Nothing is more comforting than to know that there is one in heaven who stands between you and God the Father Almighty, one who understands, who knows all there is to know about you. Jesus the man knows your faults, he knows about your feelings of guilt, he knows things about you that you don't want anybody else to know lest he or she rejects you. Jesus knows and he is even touched with feelings of compassion.

God gave John a vision so he might have a deeper insight into the person of Jesus. If you were to see him looking like an ordinary man, that in itself would not reveal his person, for you would *only* see a man. When Jesus was on this earth there was nothing about him that would cause you to stop and notice him. Many people are probably far more attractive to look at, or more striking in appearance than Jesus was. Indeed, he was so inconspicuous that when the officials wanted to arrest him, Judas, who betrayed him, arranged to give them a signal: 'The one I kiss is the man; arrest him' (Matt. 26:48). So when God gave John this vision, it was in apocalyptic language, using analogy and metaphor to draw attention to the deeper truth about Jesus that seeing him only in human form would hide. We must bear in mind that it was a vision.

Second, we need to note that John describes that vision but does not try to interpret it. However, Jesus himself interprets part of the vision, for he says in Revelation 1:20, 'The mystery of the seven stars that you saw in my right hand and of the seven golden lampstands is this: The seven stars are the angels of the seven churches, and the seven lampstands are the seven churches.' That is as far as we get in having an infallible interpretation of the vision.

The third thing to see is that the vision focuses on one person. John told us it was one 'like a son of man'. The person is identified before the vision ends. 'When I saw him, I fell at his feet as though dead. Then he placed his right hand on me and said: "Do not be afraid. I am the First and the Last. I am the Living One; I was dead, and behold I am alive for ever and ever! And I hold the keys of death and Hades"' (Rev. 1:17–18). We know that person is the Lord Jesus Christ.

It is possible that this vision answers the question 'Who is Jesus?' in a way that is truly unique. John described what he saw, but he does not tell us what he understood the vision to mean. There is a fundamental truth here: Christianity is conveyed by description, by one describing to another what he or she saw and experienced. This is the essence of Christianity. It is not a philosophy or a science, it is neither rational nor irrational, it is *supra*rational – beyond reason.

This is why Christianity confounds some people; they imagine it is something that they can grasp like any other subject. For example, an architect reads books on architecture and understands the history, descriptions and language relating to that subject. The philosopher understands great thinkers such as Plato, Aristotle and Descartes. The scientist can deal with complicated laboratory experiments and with matters that are beyond the comprehension of most of us. Yet when it comes to understanding Christianity, and they try to reduce it to an intellectual level, these people stumble. Understanding the person of Jesus is not an academic question, it is not a scientific question, it is not a philosophical question, and those who try to isolate Jesus, to put him in a test tube, as it were, or try to grasp him phenomenologically, as they do other things, will never discover who Jesus is.

John 9:1–41 tells the story of the young man who was blind from birth, but when Jesus touched his eyes he was healed. This ought to have been grounds for great rejoicing. But when the Pharisees heard about it, they reacted with great hostility. They questioned the young man angrily about the identity of the one who had healed him. Now this young man was not a theologian, or a scientist, or a philosopher. The only way he could answer their questions was to report what he knew. So he replied, 'One thing I do know. I was blind but now I see!' (v. 25).

Now that is what I mean by witness: describing your experience to another. This is the offence of Christianity, for people, by nature, want rational, intellectual, tangible evidence. Many people in Corinth rejected the gospel. Paul wrote to the Corinthian church, telling them not to be surprised at this.

> Jews demand miraculous signs and Greeks look for wisdom, but we preach Christ crucified: a stumbling-block to Jews and foolishness to Gentiles, but to those whom God has called, both Jews and Greeks, Christ the power of God and the wisdom of God (1 Cor. 1:22–24).

The wisdom of God and Christianity is this: it is receiving the word from one person who describes his or her encounter with Jesus. Christianity is a description of what we have seen by faith. Moreover, it is the Holy Spirit who reveals the answer to the question 'Who is Jesus?' This is why it is not an academic matter nor a philosophical problem.

John now describes what he saw. The first things he noticed were the seven lampstands. He said, 'I turned around to see the voice that was speaking to me. And when I turned I saw seven golden lampstands' (Rev. 1:12). Remember that John has given us the interpretation of the seven lampstands. He said, 'The seven lampstands are the seven churches' (v.20).

Now why did John see the lampstands first? The answer is this: Christianity is the church, and the answer to the question 'Who is Jesus?' is found only in the church. Does it surprise you that the first thing John sees is the church and that Jesus is the one inseparably joined to his church? This is why Christianity is offensive: Jesus is not somebody whom you can understand in isolation; he is always joined to the church. You cannot be a secret follower of Jesus. If you become a Christian, you must be identified with him. Salvation is revealed when what happens inside a person is confessed openly.

Perhaps you want to believe upon Jesus Christ secretly, because you are afraid your friends and family will ridicule you or even disown you. But the secret belief you may have in Jesus Christ *must* be confessed openly, otherwise you show that your faith is not really in the Jesus of the Bible, for Jesus Christ came as both Saviour and Lord.

Let me explain what that means: Jesus is Saviour because everything God demands of you, Jesus has already done for you. God has a very high standard, and if you are to go to heaven and avoid eternal condemnation, you must attain perfect righteousness. By this, I do not mean having good intentions or being sincere, I mean God requires that you conform to his word, to his truth, to his law, in thought, word and deed. It means if you ever have an evil thought, you destroy your chance of getting into heaven. It does not have to be an overt sin: jealousy, anger and pride are also obnoxious in God's sight.

Another kind of sin is equally repugnant to him: the sin of thinking you have not sinned and therefore do not need a Saviour. We call it self-righteousness. Now you may think you are not guilty of that because you believe 'self-righteous' is a word that describes 'Holy Joes', pious people, who go to church every time the door is open. But I want you to see how subtle self-righteousness is. The fact that you think this betrays how self-righteous you are. That is sin; therefore, you need a Saviour. You need somebody to do for you what you cannot do.

The wonderful news is that Jesus has done everything for you. He lived a sinless life, and when they crucified him he became your substitute and owned your guilt as though he committed those sins himself. God, then, poured out his wrath on his Son. Jesus was punished in your stead. Receiving him as Saviour means that you recognize your guilt and that you cannot attain the righteousness God requires, and in fact must stop trying. Martin Luther once said, 'Did we in our own strength confide, our striving would be losing.' You need to see the folly of trusting yourself and step back and marvel that Jesus did what you could not do.

However, as well as accepting Jesus as your Saviour, you must also receive him as Lord. This means you must be identified with the church for which Christ died. God wants a witness in the world and he is calling you to declare yourself openly. It means that you are not ashamed to admit that you are his and you are not ashamed to own his cause. It means that you are willing for the Son of God to do what he pleases with your life. Jesus said, 'If anyone is ashamed of me and my words, the Son of Man will be ashamed of him when he comes in his glory' (Luke 9:26). So if you are persuaded in your heart, then confess him before others. He has promised that some day you will be a co-heir with him and that he will confess you before the Father (Rom. 8:17).

The Son of God will some day be crowned King of kings, and Lord of lords. It is not a question of *whether* you are going to recognize Jesus is Lord; it is only a question of *when*. '"As surely as I live," says the Lord, "every knee will bow before me; every tongue will confess to God"' (Rom. 14:11). Confess him now and identify with others who do, and Jesus will grow more precious to you every day. Like the young man who was cured of his blindness, you will say, 'I was blind but now I see!' (John 9:25).

14

Who is Jesus? – Pre-eminent in the Church

Revelation 1:12–13

We have seen that we cannot discover who Jesus is by using academic or scientific methods; we find the answer only in the Bible, the book that made him known in the first place. Furthermore, we can only understand who Jesus is with the aid of the same Spirit that inspired men to write about him in the Bible. We cannot know who Jesus is by our natural understanding.

I want us to take a closer look at John's vision of Jesus Christ being at the centre of the seven churches. I want us to understand that in answering the question 'Who is Jesus?' we must see him as the *pre-eminence* of the church. The head of the church is not the Pope; the centre of the church is not the Eucharist; the head and the centre of the church is Jesus Christ. Therefore we must never entertain the idea of finding salvation unless we identify with the church, the visible body of Christ. We must go beyond seeing a building and the people in it, and see him who is the church's head and the centre.

Almost every week somebody comes to the vestry of Westminster Chapel and asks to become a member. I ask them certain questions and I do not always accept them as members, not because of how they look or act, but because I want to know what is their hope of salvation; I want to know why they think they are going to heaven. My point is this: you can come into the church building and attend the services, but it does you no good if you do not see Jesus, the centre and the head of the church, he who truly makes the church the church.

Our Lord chose to send letters to seven churches in Asia. I don't know why he picked those seven: there were other churches in Asia, but he selected these. These seven churches are described quite painfully; it is embarrassing to read Revelation 2 and 3, and see the condition of some of these. One would think that God would not want the dirty linen to be hung out in the front garden for everybody walking by to see. Yet we are allowed to read these letters and see bizarre things happening in the name of Christianity – things that disgrace the name of Jesus Christ.

Now if you think for even a moment that it gives you some grounds of excuse to say, 'Well, don't talk to me about becoming a Christian until the church itself is straightened out', then you are wrong. The crucial difference between you and those in the church is this: they are going to heaven and you are not. You may think that is grossly unfair; you may want to ask if those members of the church that Christ speaks against were going to heaven. The Bible does not directly answer that question; all we need to know is that God was dealing with them and God was warning them.

Maybe you look at certain churchgoers now and ask, 'How can someone like that be a Christian? They are a disgrace.' But you don't know what is happening in that person's heart; you don't know how God may be dealing with them. God *is* dealing with those in his church. The Bible says, 'Those whom I love I rebuke and discipline' (Rev. 3:19). The members of his church have this inward joy that God disciplines them: they know it is a sign of his love. The point is, there are those in the church who are being disciplined.

However, I must add one other thing: we must understand that the church is both visible and invisible. The invisible church is to be understood as those who, in the sight of God alone, are truly his own: they are the redeemed; they are those whose names are written in the Lamb's book of life, and throughout history they are drawn from every tribe and nation. These people are also part of the visible church, and we can see those of them who are alive today as they attend services and meetings week by week at their local place of worship.

The visible church, however, also includes some who are not truly God's children. The fact that you can join a church proves nothing. That, you see, would only make you a part of the visible church. I would not like to think that people could deceive me in the vestry and become members of Westminster Chapel unless they truly belong to Jesus. Yet that could happen; I am not a little pope, deciding who is saved; I use my best judgment and recommend those who give evidence based upon Scripture that they are redeemed. Nevertheless, the possibility exists that some will slip past me. The visible church may include those who are not converted.

Do you remember the parable of the ten virgins? (Matt 25:1–13). Five were wise; five were foolish, yet they had all been asked to go out and meet the bridegroom. This parable shows that not everyone in the church is right with God. Think of the parable of the wheat and the weeds (Matt 13:24–30), where we find that the wheat and the weeds were springing up together. The most meticulous minister and the most careful group of believers cannot avoid the possibility some will grow up in the church and not be regenerate. Yet there is a way of *knowing* that you are in the visible church and the invisible church, and I will tell you how before I finish this chapter.

If you become a Christian, remember that the best people will disappoint you. Many people feel inferior when they first become Christians, and they look at those who have been Christians a long time and say, 'Oh, I wish I could be as great a Christian as that!' When we are first saved, we all tend to think that everybody else is so much further along the Christian path than we are. More often than not, a young Christian will regard an older Christian as a role model. But do you know what happens every time? That person lets them down. So if you become a Christian, then come into the church with your eyes wide open. From the very beginning do not fix your eyes on others, but see Jesus in the midst of the church. He is the only one who is perfect; eventually the rest of us will disappoint you.

So in the book of Revelation God allows us to see what the church is like. The church at Ephesus had lost their first love. Christ warned them, 'If you do not repent, I will come to you and remove your lampstand from its place' (Rev. 2:5). This is what Jesus will do, for he is concerned that his church reflects his glory. One church held false doctrines; another tolerated licentiousness. The church in Sardis was proud of its reputation. God said, 'You have a reputation of being alive, but you are dead' (Rev. 3:1). The church in Laodicea was lukewarm. To them, Jesus said, 'I am about to spit you out of my mouth' (Rev. 3:16). So remember, you must come into the church with your eyes wide open. Don't ask, 'Which church is best?' Ask whether you see Jesus Christ there.

Many people seek religion in a similar fashion to those who play the stock market. I have never had enough money to do this. Nevertheless, I suppose someone with £50,000 to spend would invest £5,000 in one stock, £5,000 in another, and maybe £10,000 in one that is doing well, and so forth.

However, they never 'put all their eggs into one basket', that would be too risky. Some people look at Christianity and salvation this way; they are not sure which denomination is right, so they try this church and then they try that one, and so forth. I know of one man in America, who, in his search for religion, joined thirteen different churches and, along the way, was baptized by every conceivable method, by sprinkling, by pouring, by immersion three times forward, by immersion three times backward! 'One of these ways,' he said, 'has to be right.' He had asked the wrong question. Instead of asking, 'Which church shall I join?' he should have asked, 'Is Jesus at the centre of this church?'

I promised earlier to tell you how you can know you are in the *invisible* church, and that God sees you as one of his. This is how: you must confess Christ, you must come out of hiding, you must declare your allegiance to him. You must stake your life, your future, your final destiny on him and understand he has done everything for you that God requires. That one person is the pre-eminent Christ, the Son of Man, in the midst of the seven lampstands. Jesus came and he pleased his Father by living a perfectly obedient life. He died on a cross. In 2 Corinthians 5:21 Paul says, 'God made him who had no sin to be sin for us, so that in him we might become the righteousness of God.' God pronounced Jesus guilty because he took the punishment for our sins.

However, I end this chapter with this thought: If Christ is angry with those in his church who are not reflecting his glory, how much more angry is he with those who have never come in? Peter put it like this: 'For it is time for judgment to begin with the family of God; and if it begins with us, what will the outcome be for those who do not obey the gospel of God?' (1 Pet. 4:17). In the parable to which I referred earlier ten virgins had been invited to the wedding. Five were foolish

– a picture of those in the visible church only, and five were wise – a picture of those possibly in the visible *and* the invisible church. Are you in the visible church only, and still lost? Perhaps you have been brought up to attend church, and have even been baptized, and yet you secretly believe that it is what you *do* that counts. Remember, at the time you least expect it, God will summon you to him. The parable tells us, 'At midnight the cry rang out: "Here's the bridegroom! Come out to meet him!"' (Matt 25:6). You do not know when that day will come, but one thing is certain, when it does, the destinies of all will have been sealed, and you will pray like you never prayed in your life. 'Sir! Sir! Open the door for us!' cried the five foolish virgins. But the bridegroom replied, 'I tell you the truth, I don't know you.'

Could it be that you are in the *visible* church and God does not know you? Come to see the Christ, who is in the centre, and trust him alone. Don't leave it until it is too late.

15

Who is Jesus? – The Fulfilment of Old Testament Pictures

Revelation 1:13–15

There has been great interest in the person and work of Jesus in recent years. Like thousands of others, you may have seen *Jesus Christ Superstar* and *Godspell* – two well-known musicals that portray his life and work. Thousands more have watched films or television documentaries about him. Yet sadly, for some, this may be the only indication that Jesus existed, and perhaps their only chance to consider who he is. But the answer to the question, 'Who is Jesus?' is not found in a musical, in a film, or in a television documentary that are products of human imagination. The answer is found in the New Testament; this is our witness. The figure we see there is the true Jesus, an altogether different figure than the one portrayed by the media. He is the one you need to discover.

In the previous chapter we saw that Jesus must be regarded in terms of the inseparable connection between himself and the church. We must continue to keep this in mind. The true Jesus of the Bible reveals himself in his church; he is primarily to be found there.

Now our finite minds cannot grasp what I am about to put before you, but, humanly speaking, let us get as close as we can to the edge of eternity, before time began and the universe was created, and imagine when there was nothing except God. Had there been one speck of dust in remotest space before God, then God would not have been first. Yet *nothing* existed before God, not even empty space. We cannot imagine this, but we know that this is true. He created the universe out of nothing. The first thing Jesus said to John on that day when he was in the Spirit was this: 'I am the Alpha and the Omega [the first and the last]' (Rev. 1:8). As the first words of John's gospel tell us, 'In the beginning was the Word [Jesus], and the Word was with God, and the Word was God. He was with God in the beginning.' These verses show a Trinitarian relationship existing back in eternity. Jesus was there in the beginning.

Now the reason people cannot accept the answer they receive to the question 'Who is Jesus?' if they go to a musical like *Jesus Christ Superstar* or watch a secular documentary is that these do not show Jesus as an inseparable part of the church. However, the only Jesus that the Bible speaks of is one who came to *call out* a people to be his own. When God decided to send his Son to the earth, he had a people in mind. Hence the inseparable connection between Jesus Christ and the church. Now the word 'church' is translated from the Greek word *ekklesia*, which simply means 'the called out'. If you are a follower of Jesus Christ, you are part of the church and you are 'called out'.

When John turned to see the voice, he saw seven golden lampstands, symbolizing the seven churches that were in Asia. There is a profound truth to be grasped here: we cannot understand Jesus Christ apart from the Old Testament heritage. The Bible has two parts: the Old and the New Testaments. The Old Testament is comprised in part of God's Law, which includes most of the historical narratives which begin with the story of the patriarchs, who preceded Moses. One was Jacob, who had twelve sons. Jacob was given a new name: Israel. Thus we have the twelve sons of Israel, whose descendants grew in number to become the twelve tribes of Israel. Other kinds of literature emerged too, showing how these people thought: Wisdom literature, the Psalms, the book of Job and Proverbs. Then we have the era of the prophets, when God spoke through certain people to Israel and to all who would listen.

However, the most important thing to grasp is this: God gave Moses laws for the Children of Israel to obey: laws which include the moral law (the Ten Commandments), the ceremonial law, which detailed various ways God's people were to worship him, and the civil laws, detailing how they were to live as a community. These laws were written using a certain style of language that recurs in the New Testament. Hebrews 9 will give you a flavour of this. It may sound strange to you. For example, it speaks of the lampstand, shewbread, the veil, Aaron's rod that budded, the ark, the tables of the Covenant, cherubim and the mercy seat. 'What kind of strange, bizarre language is this?' you may ask. However, you cannot fully understand Christ until you appreciate this Old Testament heritage that preceded him.

Now the apostle Paul made an interesting statement when he tried to get the Jews and Gentiles in the early church to grasp some fundamental points regarding the Old Testament. He tried mainly to get people to see that when the law was given it was subsidiary to the promise Abraham received from God by faith. What had happened was that those to whom the law was given began to think that they were special because of their racial origin. They thought that because they were Jews and God had visited them, that automatically gave them a special place among the peoples of the world throughout history. They began to *pride* themselves on being the people of God, so Paul, who himself was a Jew, showed them that this meant nothing without faith. He raised the question of what advantage there was in being a Jew (Rom. 3:1). He tried to get them to see that what characterized the patriarchs was that they were guided by faith.

Let me give you an illustration. Often, when God blesses us in a particular way, for example, when he gives us a particular answer to prayer, we begin to think there is something special about us. What a pity! God was simply blessing us. If we begin to think like that, we are no different to those Paul spoke of in Romans 3. The same thing can happen with a nation. Take a nation that has a great history. Many would agree that God had blessed this country. But the danger is, it begins to think there is something inherently good about its national identity. The Jews felt this way, but Paul said, 'This is not so: what makes Israel special is not its racial identity, but its faith in God's promise' (see Rom. 3:27).

Now I said earlier that Christians use language that may be unfamiliar. Many hymns, for instance, use this style of language. One we sometimes sing in Westminster Chapel begins like this:

> Jesus where'er thy people meet,
> There they behold thy Mercy-seat.

William Cowper, the composer of that hymn, was not a Jew; but he was using theological language that originates in Israel's history. The Jews had been given the oracles of God and were already familiar with the terminology. But when we try to reach people today who are not Jews, we have to introduce them to theological language.

In Revelation 1 Jesus is described as in the midst of the seven golden lampstands, the *menorah*, the seven lampstands that illuminated the sanctuary. This was clearly a Jewish emblem, and was God's way of showing the continuation from the old economy to the new. It demonstrates that if you want to know who Jesus is, you must see him as the fulfilment of everything in the Old Testament.

Now we Gentiles who come to try to understand this and are introduced to this kind of terminology, will hear Jesus called the 'Lamb of God' and hear Christians speak of the 'blood of Jesus' and we may wonder what these terms mean. Well, that is Old Testament language that we must learn if we are going to make headway in understanding who Jesus is. This is why I say we must find the answer to the question 'Who is Jesus?' in the Bible. When Jesus Christ came, he was the embodiment of the laws of the Old Testament, the fulfilment of everything to which these pointed.

Let me explain the term 'mercy seat'. You may have noticed when reading Hebrews 9 that the tabernacle had two sections: in the first section were the lampstand, the shewbread and part of the sanctuary; a veil (a curtain that hung from the ceiling to the floor) separated this section from the other. On the other side of the veil was the other part of the sanctuary, the Most Holy Place. The most important object here was the mercy seat, a golden slab. Outside the tabernacle there was an altar on which the Israelites would sacrifice a goat, a calf or perhaps a lamb. Once a year the high priest would take blood from a sacrificed animal, then go behind the veil and sprinkle it on the mercy seat. Now what took place *outside* was open for all to see, but what took place *inside* was secret. Only one man, once a year, dare go behind this veil into the Most Holy Place. What took place at the altar was known as the 'offering', but what took place inside the veil was called the 'atonement'. And it was inside the veil that the most high God accepted, or did not accept, the atonement by the shedding of blood.

Then Jesus Christ came, the human embodiment of those sacrifices. Jesus became an offering when, nailed to a cross, he bore the sins of the world. But that was not the end: Jesus rose from the dead and ascended to heaven. The writer to the Hebrews shows that this heavenly ascension was the re-enactment of what had happened in the Old Testament era. It was the same as the high priest going into the Most Holy Place to sprinkle blood on the mercy seat, except that the writer to the Hebrews shows that the mercy seat is now in the heavenly sanctuary, where Jesus presented himself before the Father and where God accepted his Son's atonement.

When John sees the vision of the Son of Man, it is no accident that the *menorah* was part of his vision. It was the emblem showing again what had begun in the Old Testament, and what began when the law was given to Moses, was continuing with this difference, it is no longer on earth, but in heaven. God did not intend after Jesus came for the Mosaic law to continue, and the mercy seat, the lampstand, all prefigured the coming of Messiah.

Moreover, God had a way of affirming what his Son achieved by his sacrifice. Branded a criminal, Jesus was taken outside the city walls to be crucified. At the moment Jesus died something truly astonishing happened. Jesus said, 'It is finished' (John 19:30) and gave up his spirit, and a few hundred yards away, the veil of the temple was torn in two, split from top to bottom (Matt. 27:51). It was a terrifying sight. No human hand could have ripped it. God did it, the most high God sanctioning what his Son had done on the cross. God did not intend from that time on for the ritual atonement to continue; the material was swallowed up in the spiritual and had no place on earth.

Several hundred yards away from the site of the

crucifixion, is the Western Wall in Jerusalem, commonly known as the 'Wailing Wall'. It is all that stands now of Herod's Temple, and Jews who go there to pray, believe that they are close to the mercy seat, because just inside the wall was where the Most Holy Place was. When you visit Jerusalem, you will still find Jews vainly praying for the coming of Messiah and praying for the day when the temple will be rebuilt.

Yet the folly of the Jews today praying at the Wailing Wall is rivalled, if not exceeded, by those Christians who want to have pomp and circumstance and ritual in worship similar to what was done in ancient Israel. They have set up sanctuaries and altars and have devised all manner of ceremonies, which serve only to show they are preoccupied with the material. Churches do not need rituals, altars, statues, or burning incense: the spiritual has replaced these material emblems. Christianity is not to be seen as ceremonial and ritualistic, needing various symbols. The seat of Christianity is no longer on earth, but in heaven, and the mercy seat is at the right hand of God, and no matter where God's people meet they may see it with the eye of faith. This is what William Cowper saw when he wrote his hymn:

Jesus *where'er* thy people meet,
There they behold thy Mercy-seat [my italics].

16

Who is Jesus? – The Son of Man

Revelation 1:13–15

The Bible contains all we need to know about God and tells us all we need to know about Jesus. It is not an ordinary book. I do not say this because of its impact upon history, for in a sense that is irrelevant. The Bible is a book that is simultaneously the word of man and the word of God. You may say, 'The Bible was written by men.' You are right: the Bible was written by men, mainly by ordinary people, not necessarily all of keen minds, and we find their personalities reflected in their style of writing and reflected in what they said. You can discover the theology that lay behind their message. No sensible person would deny all this. But what you may not know is that these men wrote what they understood in proportion to their faith, and that faith was an infallible understanding of the truth.

The men God chose to write what we call the 'canon of Scripture' were men who had a greater measure of understanding than anybody since. This is why no one today could ever write with the same inspiration or infallibility. I *preach* from the Bible, but I do not *write* another Bible. Their message was written with an understanding that God gave them. That is why we say it is infallible: they wrote as the Holy Spirit moved them.

Consequently, the questions that emerge from the Bible must be answered as we get in tune with the same Holy

Spirit that moved them to write. This is a key point. In the same way that we cannot understand algebra with mathematical tools, or we cannot understand astronomy with architectural tools, we cannot understand the Bible with purely human tools.

Now we propose to answer the question 'Who is Jesus?' by using the method that will truly arrive at the answer. We call this method the 'analogy of faith'. That means we must follow the guidance of the Holy Spirit and go where he leads us, but no further. The apostle Paul put it like this: 'Think . . . with sober judgment, in accordance with the measure of faith God has given you' (Rom. 12:3). And when it comes to the gift of prophecy, Paul says that we are to prophesy according to the proportions of our faith (Rom. 12:6). The word 'proportion' is the translation of the Greek word *analogia,* which means 'analogy'. So we follow the analogy of faith.

What you may not know is that in the sixteenth century when John Calvin wrote the historic *Institutes of the Christian Religion,* acknowledged even by secular philosophers as ranking among the great publications in the history of world literature, he claimed to follow the analogy of faith. I claim to follow the analogy of faith as I preach, and it is the only method by which we can answer questions raised by the Bible. This method always involves comparing scripture with scripture, as one verse gives rise to another. And when I answer the question 'Who is Jesus?' I am not using a rational, logical method: this method is *supra*rational, *supra*logical, above reason and above logic.

The first thing I want us to see is that Jesus called himself the Son of Man; you may have noticed this and wondered why. The title 'Son of Man' was the most daring one Jesus could have assumed. One might say that it was the most presumptuous, if not the most arrogant and offensive title he *could* have assumed if he were not who he claimed to be.

There has been much speculation about why he called himself that. Some have said that calling himself the Son of Man was a sign of his humility, and he did it to avoid betraying any pride he felt in being the Son of God. But this is sentimental nonsense. Others ask why he didn't call himself the Son of God. In fact he did so frequently, far more often than many are aware. Yet more often he chose to use the audacious title 'Son of Man'. I will show you why.

We know a little about the contemporary understanding of this expression. I like to keep abreast, within reason, with modern New Testament scholarship, although I mostly take it with a grain of salt, for modern theologians are often engaged in some kind of vendetta against the historic claims of Christianity and usually form the wrong conclusions. Nevertheless, because of the discovery in 1947 and 1956 of the Dead Sea Scrolls in Qumran, modern New Testament scholarship has made a contribution I am happy to accept.

The time of Jesus and the generation just before his birth was an age in which the atmosphere was charged with the expectation of the promised Messiah. In those days the Son of Man was regarded as a divine figure who would come down from heaven, and the title 'Son of Man' was regarded as interchangeable with that of 'Messiah': those who looked for the Messiah, looked for the Son of Man. In fact, 'Son of Man' was regarded as the ultimate expression of reverence, for only God would take this title upon himself. Jesus was aware that *everybody* in contemporary Judaism knew this. So when he adopted the title, far from it being a sign of his humility, as if he were trying to disguise his deity, it showed that he regarded himself as divine.

When we read Daniel 7, it is clear that Daniel had a vision

strikingly similar to the one John had on the Isle of Patmos. He says:

> As I looked, thrones were set in place, and the Ancient of Days took his seat. His clothing was as white as snow; the hair of his head was white like wool (v. 9).

Daniel refers to God as 'the Ancient of Days', and then uses the expression 'the Son of man':

> In my vision at night I looked, and there before me was one like a son of man, coming with the clouds of heaven. He approached the Ancient of Days and was led into his presence (v. 13).

This shows the Trinitarian relationship: Daniel sees the Ancient of Days and the Son of Man as separate beings; yet if we combine what John said and what he saw and what Daniel saw we see the Trinitarian relationship. John wrote, 'In the beginning was the Word [Jesus], and the Word was with God, and the Word was God' (John 1:1).

Now we have long regarded John's Gospel as the book that, above all others, portrays the deity of Jesus. I suppose anybody would acknowledge that of the four Gospels, John's gospel shows Jesus as the Son of God in a special way. In fact, he says in John 1:34, 'I have seen and I testify that this is the Son of God.' Then in John 20:31 he tells us his purpose in writing it: 'These [things] are written that you may believe that Jesus is the Christ, the Son of God, and that by believing you may have life in his name.'

Here we notice something extremely interesting: John tells us explicitly that he wrote the Gospel that we might see Jesus as the Son of God, and yet in the Gospel of John, and in Matthew, Mark and Luke, Jesus *repeatedly* calls himself the Son of Man. Some scholars claim that the Gospels were written by men putting their own theology into the words of Jesus. But if John's purpose in writing his Gospel was to reveal Jesus to be the Son of God, why, then, did John allow the expression 'Son of Man' to remain? If these scholars are correct, why did John not substitute 'Son of God' for 'Son of Man'? The fact that he left the term 'Son of Man' in place undoubtedly proves that this is the way in which Jesus described himself.

Let us look now at John 3:12–13, which shows us by Jesus' own testimony he was indeed who he claimed to be.

> I have spoken to you of earthly things and you do not believe; how then will you believe if I speak of heavenly things? No-one has ever gone into heaven except the one who came from heaven—the Son of Man.

Here we have Jesus owning the title 'Son of Man', and you can see how he says that he is the Son of Man who came down from heaven. In John 6:62 he put it in almost the same way: 'What if you see the Son of Man ascend to where he was before!' So we clearly see that Jesus recognized the figure of the Son of Man as coming from heaven.

The second thing that I want us to see is that Jesus tells us in John 3:14 that the Son of Man was to be lifted up. 'Just as Moses lifted up the snake in the desert, so the Son of Man must be lifted up.' What we have here is a subtle, but radical, departure from the popular consensus in Jesus' day regarding what the Son of Man was to be. Jesus, in a somewhat disguised way, was saying something that would point to what he himself would do. Later, in John 12:32 he says, 'But I, when I am lifted up from the earth, will draw all men to myself.' This refers to his crucifixion.

The third thing that Jesus said about the Son of Man was this: in believing on him, we can be assured of eternal life.

Let us return to John 3:14, now adding verse 15, 'Just as Moses lifted up the snake in the desert, so the Son of Man must be lifted up, that everyone who believes in him may have eternal life.'

Here was another indication of what he was going to do, but it did not fit into the pattern of contemporary thinking. They had no idea that when the Messiah came he would be crucified, much less that he would give men and women eternal life. Nonetheless, the consensus was that the Son of Man would be a figure coming from heaven. Jesus not only owned that title, but now said other things concerning the Son of Man for which they were unprepared.

The fourth thing is this: the Son of Man and the Son of God are the same person. We need to consider this very carefully. John 3:16 says this: 'For God so loved the world that he gave his one and only Son.' Here we find Jesus using the term 'Son of God'. Remember he had just called himself the Son of Man (vv. 13, 14), but now he says, 'God so loved the world that he gave his Son.' The Son of Man, who is believed on for eternal life, is now called the one and only Son of God, who is believed on for eternal life.

Like John, Peter was a fisherman, a simple man, albeit a very colourful character with a tendency to be impetuous. But when Peter was in the Spirit, he was truly in the Spirit. On one such occasion Jesus asked Peter and his other disciples this:

'Who do people say the Son of Man is?'
    They replied, 'Some say John the Baptist; others say Elijah; and still others, Jeremiah or one of the prophets.'
    'But what about you?' he asked. 'Who do you say I am?'
    Simon Peter answered, 'You are the Christ, the Son of the living God.'
    Jesus replied, 'Blessed are you, Simon, son of Jonah, for

this was not revealed to you by man, but by my Father in heaven' (Matt. 16:13–17).

So when we come to the heart of the question 'Who is Jesus?' we realize that to see him as the Son of Man is also to see him as the Son of God.

Yet no one can reveal that to you. Nor will your natural gifts and your natural powers enable you to understand who Jesus is. This is why I said in the beginning of this chapter that I am following the only method by which one can really understand Jesus, that is by being in tune with the Holy Spirit, who moved these men to write about him. For as long as you see Jesus merely as a figure in human history, as a good man, a great man, or even as a great teacher, but no more than that, you are confirming what he said about you: you are trying to understand who he is in the context of your natural gifts, logic and reason (1 Cor. 2:14). But if you are ever elevated into a different kind of understanding, you see Jesus is more than a mere human: he is the one who came down from heaven and promised to return there.

In John 17 he prayed: 'Father, the time has come. Glorify your Son, that your Son may glorify you . . . And now, Father, glorify me in your presence with the glory I had with you before the world began' (vv. 1, 5). Jesus' prayer clearly testifies that he came from heaven. The next day the Son of Man was lifted up on a cross.

Let us look at John 3:14–15 again: 'Just as Moses lifted up the snake in the desert, so the Son of Man must be lifted up, that everyone who believes in him may have eternal life.' Jesus referred to the time when the Jews were in the Sinai desert, after God had delivered them from their bondage in Egypt. As a consequence of their constant grumbling about him and about Moses, God allowed many of them to be bitten by venomous snakes. However, when the Israelites repented, Moses prayed for them, and God said:

'Make a snake and put it up on a pole; anyone who is bitten can look at it and live.' So Moses made a bronze snake and put it up on a pole. Then when anyone was bitten by a snake and looked at the bronze snake, he lived (Num. 21:8–9).

That is all it took – a look. Imagine that.

Now the snake is symbolic of the curse that was put on men and women, because Satan used the snake in the Garden of Eden to tempt Adam and Eve, our first parents, to disobey God, and sin entered the world (Gen. 3). Because the snake tempted them, it was cursed, and to this day a snake has an eerie appearance that nobody likes. In Galatians we read: 'Cursed is everyone who is hung on a tree' (Gal. 3:13). It was in this way Jesus was lifted up – on a tree.

A common form of the death penalty the Romans used then was execution by crucifixion. They would nail the criminal through his hands and his feet to a cross. Then they would hoist the cross up and drop it into a ready-made hole in the ground. The victim would hang there until death brought a merciful release. It was not only the most shameful kind of death, but the most painful.

Nobody ever dreamed that the Son of Man, this divine figure from heaven, would die a shameful death. This is why the Jews, as a whole, have never accepted Jesus. They had a preconceived idea about what the Messiah would be like. Over the years their traditions added to Scripture, and when the Messiah came they rejected him because he did not fit into the way they interpreted it. A Messiah hanging on a cross had no place in their thinking. But it had been God's purpose all along that the Son of Man, who came down from heaven, should be crucified. On that cross Jesus is offered to all, and he has promised that all who believe on him should have everlasting life (John 3:16). Six hundred years before the event took place, the Holy Spirit revealed it to Isaiah the prophet:

> He was pierced for our transgressions, he was crushed for our iniquities; the punishment that brought us peace was upon him, and by his wounds we are healed. We all, like sheep, have gone astray, each of us has turned to his own way; and the LORD has laid on him the iniquity of us all (Isa. 53:5-6).

Look at him, and own him as your Saviour. All it takes is a look, a look at the Son of Man on the cross.

17

Who is Jesus? – The Last Adam

Revelation 1:13–15

There is more for us to see about the title 'Son of Man' – something about the person of Jesus that I think is largely overlooked. It is certainly something secular thinkers miss when they attempt to give the answer to the question 'Who is Jesus?', and it is not something that one would grasp on one's own. It is to be seen only through the revelation of the Holy Spirit. For not only does 'Son of Man' mean the God-man, who came down from heaven, it means that the Son of Man was indeed truly, physically man. Jesus was God as though he were not man, yet he was man as though he were not God. He was the second Adam, the last Adam, as he was called in 1 Corinthians 15:45.

However, before we can know who the second Adam is, we need to know something about the first Adam. God created the first Adam, the first man that ever lived, in his own likeness. Yet man fell from his first estate, and left for his posterity only a vestige of that image of God. In fact, the image of God in humanity after Adam sinned was so marred that it bears almost no resemblance to its original state.

But what about the second Adam? Well, the second Adam was not God's creation. Rather, he is the embodiment of God himself. Hence the expression 'God incarnate', meaning 'God in the flesh'. So when we are dealing with the man Jesus, we are dealing with him who was sent from heaven by God, but who, at the same time, *is* God. Theologians call Jesus the second person of the Trinity. John 1:1 says, 'In the beginning was the Word [Jesus], and the Word was with God, and the Word was God.' When Jesus came to earth, he was born of a woman, and was, thus, truly human. Not only that, this man Jesus was everything that Adam was by creation, with these exceptions: (1) he did not do what Adam did, that is, sin, and (2) he did what Adam did not do, that is, live in perfect obedience to his Father. So Scripture describes him as 'holy, blameless, pure, set apart from sinners' (Heb. 7:26).

The writer of Hebrews also describes Jesus as being one who was 'tempted in every way, just as we are—yet was without sin' (Heb. 4:15). Now some think that Jesus could not have been truly human if he did not sin, and this is what offends modern theologians. Contemporary theological opinion holds that if Jesus was really human then he must have been a sinner. It is inconceivable to 'natural' man that anyone could live a life totally free from sin. This shows how blind contemporary theologians are, for the truth is that Jesus, the Son of Man, was uniquely true man, and he was true man *because* he never sinned.

God does not see us in this way: our heritage is retroactive to that first Adam. He sinned, and the whole human race sinned with him. You may say, 'Well, I was not there when Adam sinned, and I am an individual. I don't have to go the way he did.' All I can say to you is 'Do you live in perfect obedience to your heavenly Father? Are you without sin? No. So by the way you live, you show you *were* there. You are no different to the first Adam.' Jesus was uniquely, truly human: he was all God meant humans to be. If you want to know what we were supposed to be like, look at Jesus.

The man and the woman in God's original creation were

innocent, endowed with perfection, and with perfect morality. However, God also gave them a free will. He created them, as Augustine put it, 'able to sin', and then, after Adam and Eve fell, everyone born was not able *not* to sin. Jesus Christ, the Son of Man, the second Adam, came to this earth and did what Adam failed to do. And it is only when men and women are joined to Christ that they are enabled not to sin. One day we will be glorified and then we will be totally unable to sin. The cycle will be complete.

We dealt briefly with Adam's sin in an earlier chapter, but we need to look at the account in greater detail at this point. The story goes like this:

> Now the serpent was more crafty than any of the wild animals the Lord God had made. He said to the woman, 'Did God really say, "You must not eat from any tree in the garden"?' (Gen. 3:1).

Satan, in the form of this serpent, lied; God had *not* said, 'You must not eat from *any* tree in the garden.' The serpent was dealing with Eve in a subtle way. But, more important, his strategy was to make her doubt what God had said. Here is an important lesson: the first way the devil tempts us is to make us doubt God's word. We all need to remember this, for we have an enemy who is an extremely self-concealing being. If you do not believe in the devil, he has succeeded with you, for that is precisely what he wants you to believe. The apostle Paul gave the devil a nickname, calling him 'the god of this age [who] has blinded the minds of unbelievers, so that they cannot see the light of the gospel of the glory of Christ, who is the image of God' (2 Cor. 4:4). And we see the first thing the devil did when he came to Eve was to tempt her to doubt what God had said.

Then Eve began to converse with Satan:

The woman said to the serpent, 'We may eat fruit from the trees in the garden, but God did say, "You must not eat fruit from the tree that is in the middle of the garden, and you must not touch it, or you will die."'

'You will not surely die,' the serpent said to the woman. 'For God knows that when you eat of it your eyes will be opened, and you will be like God, knowing good and evil' (Gen. 3:2–5).

Now, the woman began to succumb to reason. This is the next ploy that Satan adopts: he appeals to your reason as he did with Eve. Then, when she succumbed to this way of thinking, Satan confirmed her reasoning was right. It is an extraordinary thing, but once you doubt God's word and opt for reason instead, you will always receive confirmation that appears to justify the stance you wish to adopt. Yet that very confirmation is simply to keep you blind indefinitely.

When the woman saw that the fruit of the tree was good for food and pleasing to the eye, and also desirable for gaining wisdom, she took some and ate it. She also gave some to her husband, who was with her, and he ate it (Gen. 3:6).

Eve was satisfied she had done the right thing. This is the way the devil works: he will get you to doubt God's word; he will put reason in its place, and he will give you confirmation, so that you take the wrong route, although you are completely satisfied you have done the right thing. This is the way the devil keeps men and women bound and blinded.

Now let us consider the second Adam. He had a similar experience to that of the first Adam, although the outcome was different. The same devil who succeeded with the first Adam came to tempt the second Adam. Matthew 4:1–3 says:

Then Jesus was led by the Spirit into the desert to be tempted by the devil. After fasting forty days and forty nights, he was hungry. The tempter came to him and said, 'If you are the Son of God, tell these stones to become bread.'

The devil employed the same subtle tactics he always uses to make a person doubt. In saying, '*If* you are the Son of God', he implied Jesus might not be, and so he tried to make Jesus, who was in a weakened condition owing to his long fast, question his relationship to his Father. But Jesus replied:

'It is written: "Man does not live on bread alone, but on every word that comes from the mouth of God"' (Matt. 4:4).

When we compare the temptation of the first Adam with the temptation of Jesus, the second Adam, we can already see one difference: the first Adam succumbed, while the second Adam resisted the devil. However, the devil does not give up easily, and he thought he would try again. This time the devil took Jesus into the holy city, Jerusalem and led him to the pinnacle of the temple, high above the ground.

'If you are the Son of God,' he said, 'throw yourself down. For it is written: "He will command his angels concerning you, and they will lift you up in their hands, so that you will not strike your foot against a stone"' (Matt. 4:6).

Satan quoted from Psalm 91:11–12, which is a reminder that the devil knows the Bible well and will even quote Scripture when tempting us to do wrong. Has this happened to you? Have you looked for a reason to confirm your behaviour and found a verse of Scripture that seems to justify your point of view?

> Jesus answered, 'It is also written: Do not put the Lord your God to the test' (Matt. 4:7).

But the devil did not give up and tried again.

> Again, the devil took him to a very high mountain and showed him all the kingdoms of the world and their splendour. 'All this I will give you,' he said, 'if you will bow down and worship me.'
>
> Jesus said to him, 'Away from me, Satan! For it is written: Worship the Lord your God and serve him only.'
>
> Then the devil left him, and angels came and attended him (Matt. 4:8-11).

Now this is just one example that I give to show the difference between the first Adam and the second Adam. The first Adam failed and gave in to temptation: the second Adam succeeded and resisted the devil. This is what I mean by Jesus being truly human. To put it another way: by the way he lived, Jesus displayed authentic manliness. If you want to see a real man, then look at Jesus. We are the cowards, ones who succumb, weaklings. He was truly human and came to be what we are not.

We are living in a very strange time in human history. It is a time when role reversals become increasingly commonplace. Men are becoming more feminine and women are becoming more rugged and masculine. This is partly owing to the breakdown of the family unit. For when boys are raised by a single parent, especially by the mother, there is sometimes a distorted sexual identification. The same is true if a girl is raised by a father. A whole generation now has been brought up in broken homes. Real manliness, true womanhood, is rapidly declining. Today women want to 'wear the trousers', and, surprisingly, the men are quite happy for them to be heads of the household. Real manliness nowadays is rare. But if you want to see a man look at Jesus.

We are told that he learned obedience through suffering. Unlike Jesus, you and I want things easy, to avoid pain and suffering, and when it comes to temptation it is so often easier to succumb than to resist. I know the temptations young people experience. I can recall how, when I was growing up, that it was regarded as the manly thing to do this or to do that. The real man, or the real woman, is the one who resists temptation. If you want to be a real woman, accept yourself as God created you: you are a weaker vessel. That is the way God made you.

The only way that we can find our true identity is to conform to God's word. Do you want to be a real man? Do you want to be a real woman? Then become joined to the one who invites you to be all he is. You may ask, 'How do I begin?' Don't begin with yourself. When you do that you will immediately begin to justify yourself. 'Behold the man!' said Pontius Pilate, when he confessed before the crowd, 'I find no fault in him' (John 19:5, 6 AV). Look at Jesus. Look at him, who was obedient, pure, clean, whole — all that God wanted humanity to be. Look at Jesus. See him as pure, clean, undefiled and obedient. Then look at yourself, undone, vile, guilty and naked.

Follow Jesus as he walks the shores of Galilee, having compassion on the crowds and forgiving sin. Follow him all the way to Gethsemane, where, as a man, he prayed, 'Father, if you are willing, take this cup from me; yet not my will, but yours be done' (Luke 22:42). Follow him all the way to Calvary. Look at the man Jesus hoisted up from the earth on that cruel wooden cross. Listen, as he cries, 'Father, forgive them, for they do not know what they are doing' (Luke 23:34). Listen as, at the point of death, Jesus says, 'It is finished', and gives up his spirit (John 19:30). He has accomplished everything his Father asked.

That is not the end. Jesus rose from the dead and ascended to heaven. This is where he is now, ruling from his throne. The apostle Paul describes him like this: 'There is one God and one mediator between God and men, the man Christ Jesus, who gave himself as a ransom for all men' (1 Tim. 2:5). You need that mediator. Don't try to clothe yourself with your reason, with your self-justification, but come to see your nakedness, and to see that you need what the second Adam alone can do for you. Come to see him, the second Adam, who must mediate between you and your Father, for, like the first Adam, you have failed.

By the way there will be no 'third' Adam. The second Adam was the 'last Adam' (1 Cor. 15:45). There will be no others.

The man Jesus is coming again. The apostle Paul describes the day when he says:

> For the Lord himself will come down from heaven, with a loud command, with the voice of the archangel and with the trumpet call of God, and the dead in Christ will rise first. After that, we who are still alive and are left will be caught up together with them in the clouds to meet the Lord in the air. And so we will be with the Lord forever (1 Thess. 4:16-17).

I don't know when he is coming, but when he does come, that will be the end. *Then*, he alone will be your judge. Are you ready to meet him?

18

Who is Jesus? – Our Great High Priest

In this chapter we continue to look at the way John describes Jesus in his vision. Jesus was dressed, we are told, in 'a robe reaching down to his feet and with a golden sash around his chest' (Rev. 1:13). In this description we see things that are profound.

The first is that the vision reveals the priesthood of Jesus. The idea of priesthood goes back to the book of Exodus in the Old Testament, when God gave Aaron these instructions:

> Tell all the skilled men to whom I have given wisdom in such matters that they are to make garments for Aaron, for his consecration, so he may serve me as priest. These are the garments they are to make: a breastpiece, an ephod, a robe, a woven tunic, a turban and a sash. They are to make these sacred garments for your brother Aaron and his sons, so they may serve me as priests (Exod. 28:3–4).

Jesus, then, is dressed in a similar way to the high priests of the Old Testament, and in this vision we are reminded of his priestly office.

Nowadays, perhaps too often the debate regarding the question 'Who is Jesus?' centres almost exclusively on the question of his deity or his manhood; what is often overlooked is his function. However, to understand who he is, we must see what he did and does.

Now what was the function of the high priest? First, we must look again at his sacrificial role in making the sin-offering in the temple. (You may recall we discussed this in

Chapter 5.) The high priest would take a lamb, a goat, or a calf, and after slaughtering it, he would offer it on the altar in the temple. Then he would take the blood from that animal and go behind the veil and enter the Most Holy Place. There, he would sprinkle the blood on the mercy seat and God ratified the atonement for Israel's sins. The writer of Hebrews describes the Day of Atonement like this:

> Only the high priest entered the inner room, and that only once a year, and never without blood, which he offered for himself and for the sins the people had committed in ignorance. The Holy Spirit was showing by this that the way into the Most Holy Place had not yet been disclosed as long as the first tabernacle was still standing. . . . He [Jesus] did not enter by means of the blood of goats and calves; but he entered the Most Holy Place once for all by his own blood, having obtained eternal redemption (Heb. 9:7–8, 12).

Jesus Christ came as high priest (v. 11) and made atonement for our sin by shedding his blood on the cross, thus becoming the offering for us all. Being sinless, he did not make atonement for himself, but he offered himself in our place. Forty days after Jesus rose from the dead, he ascended into heaven and took his seat at God's right hand. There he remains, our ongoing substitute, as it were, though not in the sense of continually offering himself, for he had done that 'once for all' (Heb. 7:27). With his own blood, for all eternity, Jesus perfectly satisfied the justice of God. Not only that, Hebrews 10:13 tells that he sat down until his enemies become his footstool. So we see that the role of the high priest in the Old Testament was transferred to Jesus. However, there is something about this high priest that is different. Hebrews 4:15 says, 'We do not have a high priest who is unable to sympathise with our weaknesses, but we have one who has been tempted in every way, just as we are—yet was without sin.' This is an extraordinary statement: we have a high priest who is compassionate. You see, the high priest in the Old Testament had to offer atonement for his own sins, and so was unable to be sympathetic to others. He was concerned about himself, that he too would be forgiven, that he too would be the object of God's grace, and that God would ratify the atonement for his sin. Jesus, our High Priest, is indeed different: he understands everything and feels concern for us.

Have you been touched by feelings of compassion for others? If so, then, the chances are you can only *truly* sympathize with somebody who has the same problems as you. It is harder to commiserate with someone who does not share your difficulties. Let me give you an example. If you are of the tradition where you confess your sins to a priest, you may do this, and feel better because you feel the priest is listening and you have confessed everything. An interesting story about Martin Luther is that he often left the confessional booth believing he had confessed everything, only to return an hour later, remembering something else. Sometimes he would return two or three times in the same day. His confessors began to pass him around saying, 'Here he comes again. Well, you take him this time. I no longer have the heart to listen.' The truth is, the best of us can only sympathize if we have shared the same experience. The extraordinary thing about Jesus is that he faced the same temptations as we face, and we have no problem, no weakness or infirmity that does not touch him.

Let me give you a further illustration. When I was seventeen years old, my mother passed away. This was a most traumatic experience, and I doubt whether I have ever really recovered. It was also a deeply unhappy time for my father. I will never forget being at the funeral home, where different people were coming by to offer their sympathy. (People usually remember to be sympathetic for the time of the funeral, or maybe for a week or two afterwards. Nevertheless, people are human and soon they forget, while we, who have gone through death and sorrow, are affected by grief for months after.) My father sat in the corner of the room, and remained seated because to stand as so many offered condolences would have tired him. Then I noticed my father spontaneously rising to his feet and I wondered why. Coming into the room was a man who caught my father's attention and he thought, 'Here is someone who *understands* how I feel.' Then they embraced and wept on each other's shoulders. You see, that man had lost *his* wife two weeks before and so they had this experience in common. This man was truly touched with feelings of compassion.

Now, this high priest, Jesus Christ, is like that: he understands and is touched by your weakness, your problems and your sense of despair. Who is Jesus? He is the one who was tried, who was tempted at all points as we are. No matter what your problem is, how strange, how unusual, how extraordinary, Jesus understands. Where can you find somebody like that? Where can you find one who will weep with you? When Lazarus died, on seeing his sister Mary's tears, 'Jesus wept' (John 11:35). He wept with those who were weeping, he wept with those who had a sense of loss, even weeping with those who were angry with him for not arriving in time to prevent Lazarus' death. Have you ever asked the questions, 'If God is in heaven, why does he allow evil to continue in the world? Why are there so many tragedies and so much pain and suffering? Surely if God is all-powerful he can intervene?' Jesus understands how you feel, because precisely the same charges were put to him.

'Lord, by not being here, you are responsible for our brother's death. You could have been here and you could have stopped it, but you didn't come.' Perhaps, theological questions about suffering and tragic events you are unable to understand have kept you from seeking God. Our high priest Jesus understands that and his reaction is to weep.

Why God permits these things is the most difficult question in the world. But I must remind you that there is something else you should know: if God gave you the correct abstract answers to those questions, you would no longer need faith. Do you think God is ignorant that this is the question everybody asks? God *knows* this is on our mind, and, as we saw, it was put to Jesus himself and he wept because he understands.

I want to ask you this: who do you know like that? Who do you know who would be touched by your weaknesses like he is? When I was a boy, we used to sing this chorus:

> Standing somewhere in the shadows you'll find Jesus;
> He is the only one who cares and understands.
> Standing somewhere in the shadows you'll find Jesus,
> And you'll know him by the nail prints in his hands.

There is another thing that I want us to see about Jesus, as our high priest. This description is that of a warrior going to battle. This is not accidental, for the one sweeping description 'dressed in a robe reaching down to his feet and with a golden sash round his chest' simultaneously describes the high priest and the Son of God, who goes forth to war. Hebrews 10:12–13 says:

> But when this priest had offered for all time one sacrifice for sins, he sat down at the right hand of God. Since that time he waits for his enemies to be made his footstool.

So, as the Son of Man, Jesus is what the Old Testament high priest could not be: he is simultaneously God and man, uniquely true man, and, as our warrior, he is the defender of the church, and one day will make his enemies his footstool.

We may ask who are his enemies? I think we can give three categories.

First, his enemies are any who are enemies of his people. For example, the apostle Paul put it like this: 'God is just: he will pay back trouble to those who trouble you' (2 Thess. 1:6). We are dealing with the same compassionate man, who sympathizes with our weaknesses, but now we see another side of his nature, however, one that is consistent. One of the great fringe benefits in being a Christian is that Jesus Christ fights our battles; he regards it as right to avenge those who are his. '"It is mine to avenge; I will repay," says the Lord' (Rom. 12:19). Vengeance is not something that we take upon ourselves; God does it. And your enemies become his enemies if you are truly his.

The second enemy is the devil. One thing that new Christians soon learn is that they not only gain a new friend, but they also gain a new enemy, Satan. Peter describes Satan as 'a roaring lion looking for someone to devour' (1 Pet. 5:8). Until you become a Christian, his task is to keep you in the state of spiritual blindness, blind to your own condition, blind to the fact that you have grieved a holy God, blind to the knowledge that your heart is 'deceitful above all things and beyond cure' (Jer. 17:9), blind to the fact that you need a mediator, and blind to the fact that there is a heaven and there is a hell.

The wonderful thing is that we have victory over the devil now, through the blood that Jesus shed on the cross, but not only that, the Bible says that some day the devil will be cast into the lake of fire. Indeed, Jesus told us that the devil was the reason hell was created in the first place (Matt. 25:41).

There is one more enemy to consider at this point: death. Paul tells us in 1 Corinthians 15:26: 'The last enemy to be destroyed is death.' Death was destroyed by the blood Jesus shed on the cross, and at the resurrection of the dead on the last day everyone will see the actuality of this. It does not matter whether they were buried in a tomb centuries ago, or have been cremated in the twentieth century, for God, by his Spirit, will bring everybody to life and death will be swallowed up in victory (1 Cor. 15:54). Until then, Jesus will be at the right hand of God, the high priest, who is the warrior, the defender of his people, the conqueror of the devil, and, in the end, of death itself.

However, the Bible speaks of the second death, which is this: after our first death and the final resurrection, God will bring us back to stand trial at the Judgment. If our names are not written in the Lamb's book of life, we will be consigned to that place of outer darkness, called the second and eternal death (Rev. 21:8).

Are you ready to face God in that Final Judgment? How do you feel at the thought of standing before the Almighty God on that day? I must tell you that unless you are a Christian the greatest friend you can ever have, the one who views your feelings of loss, your weaknesses and all your problems with compassion is the same Jesus who, on that day, will be your worst enemy. The enemy you gain when you become a Christian, the devil, is nothing compared to having to face the Son of God on the Day of Judgment.

The Bible tells us 'Jesus wept' (John 11:35), and he weeps with us now. But another emotion is attributed to the same God: laughing. This kind of laughter is unfamiliar to us. We can read about it, however, in Proverbs 1:24-29, where God says:

'Since you rejected me when I called and no-one gave heed when I stretched out my hand, since you ignored all my advice and would not accept my rebuke, I in turn will laugh at your disaster; I will mock when calamity overtakes you—when calamity overtakes you like a storm, when disaster sweeps over you like a whirlwind, when distress and trouble overwhelm you. Then they will call to me but I will not answer; they will look for me but will not find me. Since they hated knowledge and did not choose to fear the Lord.'

In Psalm 2:12 we read these words: 'Kiss the Son, lest he be angry.' Remember, in the description of the Son of Man in John's vision we have simultaneously the description of the high priest touched with feelings of sympathy, and of the Son of God, who goes to war and is determined to punish his enemies. The same Son of Man, who regards you now with such compassion, will some day become the worst enemy you have ever known, for it is he who will consign you to everlasting hell.

But Jesus came as high priest, and all the sins that we have ever committed were charged to him, and God pronounced him guilty instead of us. No greater injustice, no greater indignity can be hurled at him than not to believe on him. This is why the psalmist said, 'Kiss the Son, lest he be angry' (Ps. 2:12). You may ask, 'How do I kiss him?' I will answer: confess him, recognize that all the punishment you deserve was placed upon him as your high priest, and then show you are not ashamed to own him as your Saviour and your Lord. Then you will not need to fear; in fact, there is such a thing as having boldness in the Day of Judgment, for Jesus said, 'Whoever acknowledges me before men, I will also acknowledge him before my Father in heaven' (Matt. 10:32).

19

Who is Jesus? – The King

Revelation 1:12–13

One of the most sublime and most important things about
Jesus in John's vision is that not only is he the Son of Man
and our great high priest, but he is also King. The sash around
his chest in Revelation 1:13 is an explicit reference to his
kingship. Indeed, the accusation that he claimed to be King
of the Jews was hurled at Jesus at his trial (Matt. 27:11;
Luke 23:3). Jesus accepted the claim and the New Testament
clearly portrays him as our King (Matt. 2:2; Luke 19:38;
John 1:49; 12:13; Acts 17:7; 1 Tim. 1:17; 6:15; Rev. 15:3;
17:14; 19:16).

Now we begin this chapter by looking at the story of Adam
and Eve. We learn in Genesis 3 that when God created them
they were naked. Yet it was not until after they sinned that
they became aware of this (vv. 7, 10). When Jesus, the Son
of God, came he was sinless from the beginning. But he
clothed himself as a further symbol of taking upon himself
the likeness of our sinful flesh.

Furthermore, his acceptance of the role of king was even
a great humiliation for him, for if you know anything about
the history of Israel, and how the notion of kingship came
into being, you will know it was never God's intention for
Israel to have a king. But the time came when Israel pleaded
for a monarch. Samuel, the prophet of God at that time, said
to them, 'God does not want you to have a king.'

But the people refused to listen to Samuel. 'No!' they said. 'We want a king over us. Then we will be like all the other nations, with a king to lead us and to go out before us and fight our battles.'

When Samuel heard all that the people said, he repeated it before the LORD. The LORD answered, 'Listen to them and give them a king' (1 Sam. 8:19–22).

Because of the hardness of their hearts, God accommodated Israel and made Saul their king, but he was angry and displeased. Saul was a man who was gifted at administration and things of that nature, but he did not truly know the Lord intimately and later God rejected him. In Hosea 13:11 God said, 'In my anger I gave you a king, and in my wrath I took him away.'

However, God then raised up another king, a man 'after his own heart' (1 Sam. 13:14). His name was David. Then we have the long line of the kings of Israel and Judah before the royal line seemed to disappear. At last, the time came when God sent the angel Gabriel to the virgin Mary to tell her she was going to have a son whom she was to name Jesus. He said, 'He will be great and will be called the Son of the most High. The Lord God will give him the throne of his father David' (Luke 1:32).

So when God sent his Son into the world, he was not only clothed in the likeness of sinful humanity but held the title of king. Yet those to whom Jesus was sent never recognized him as the King of Israel. John 1:10–11 tells us, 'He was in the world, and though the world was made through him, the world did not recognise him. He came to that which was his own, but his own did not receive him.' Furthermore, because of what Jesus said the Jews hated him and, deciding he was a fraud, an impostor who deserved death, they crucified him.

They justified their deed like this: 'The people stood watching, and the rulers even sneered at him. They said, "He saved others; let him save himself if he is the Christ of God, the Chosen One"' (Luke 23:35). In other words, they were quite happy for him to prove himself to be all he claimed. That he did not save himself on the cross justified their actions and cleared them of any guilt. And so they mocked him. Nailed to the post above Jesus' head was the placard stating the crime for which he was executed. Pontius Pilate, the Roman Governor, had written in Greek, Latin and Hebrew, 'THIS IS THE KING OF THE JEWS' (Luke 23:38). The Jews had protested about the wording of this sign to Pilate:

> 'Do not write "The King of the Jews", but that this man claimed to be king of the Jews.' Pilate answered, 'What I have written, I have written' (John 19:21–22).

My point is that this was the charge against him, that Jesus was the King of the Jews.

Now since Jesus was indeed the King of the Jews and assumed that role of kingship, what was the nature of his kingdom? This is what the Jews never understood, for 'natural' man can *never* grasp this. Jesus said that his kingdom was spiritual. As he stood before Pilate, he said, 'My kingdom is not of this world. If it were, my servants would fight to prevent my arrest by the Jews. But now my kingdom is from another place' (John 18:36).

The curse of Judaism to this very day may be summed up like this: the Jews were never able to see beyond the physical. Yet this is not limited to the Jewish mind alone: this is the way all men and women are by nature; they can never see beyond the physical; they can never see the analogy of faith. The Holy Spirit alone enables one to do this. Jesus did not match their expectations and they rejected him. So will you if you demand that he match your idea of a Saviour. The question is, will you see what the Jews never saw? Will you see what the secular man cannot see? Jesus made it clear: his kingdom is a *spiritual* realm. Moreover, it is a kingdom that would be ruled from heaven. The psalmist saw it hundreds of years before Jesus came: 'The Lord says to my Lord: "Sit at my right hand until I make your enemies a footstool for your feet" ' (Ps. 110:1).

The cross was not the end; the Bible says that Jesus rose from the dead. However, that too is something revealed by the Holy Spirit. This is why the apostle Paul wrote: 'If you confess with your mouth, "Jesus is Lord," and believe in your heart that God raised him from the dead, you will be saved' (Rom. 10:9). Once the Spirit reveals this, you will be unshakeable in your belief. Yet the extraordinary thing is, to those whom the Holy Spirit has revealed it, it is so clear that they sometimes cannot understand why others cannot see it.

After his resurrection Jesus appeared to his followers at various times. Paul tells us that more than five hundred people saw him (1 Cor. 15:6). Then, after forty days, he ascended to heaven and fulfilled the oracle in Psalm 110:1: 'Sit at my right hand until I make your enemies a footstool for your feet.' The New Testament, in fact, speaks perhaps a dozen times, of Jesus being seated at the right hand of God. That is where he is now, ruling his kingdom. In doing this, Jesus (1) protects his kingdom, and (2) he guarantees its growth in the world – growth that is guaranteed through the gifts that are given to those who are in the church and through those who are added to it. To put it another way: as Sovereign, King Jesus determines who enters his church. Whatever else can be said about a sovereign, one thing is certain, he alone has the right to determine who enters his presence.

Now, before Jesus returned to heaven, he showed how we might enter his presence. Speaking to Nicodemus, he put it like this: 'I tell you the truth, no-one can see the kingdom of God unless he is born again.'

Nicodemus replied, 'How can a man be born when he is old? Surely he cannot enter a second time into his mother's womb to be born!'

'No,' Jesus said, 'You must be born of the Spirit' (John 3:3–5).

Now one thing is certain about your own physical birth: you had nothing to do with your arrival into this world – it happened. The new birth is the same: in your own strength, you have nothing to do with it. There are two reasons for this. The first is, there must be the birth of the Spirit if you are to see the kingdom of God. Here, to 'see' means to see beyond the physical, to grasp spiritually. This comes through the Holy Spirit, because (1) by nature, you can never see it; it is preposterous to the 'natural' mind, and (2) Jesus, who is now at the right hand of God, sovereignly determines who enters his kingdom. In his prayer in John 17 Jesus referred to the glory that he had with the Father before the world began and said, 'Glorify your Son, that your Son may glorify you. For you granted him authority over all people that he might give eternal life to all those you have given him' (vv. 1, 2). Jesus, on the throne, is the one who gives eternal life. The kingdom is a spiritual kingdom and we can enter it only through the Holy Spirit.

Now I must tell another thing about the kingship of Jesus: what some of us now see so clearly by faith, some day everybody will see by sight. The worst thing that can ever happen to you is to number among the latter. 'Prove what you are saying,' you may demand. I cannot prove it. The apostle Paul struggled against the problem of their unbelief when he dealt with the Corinthians, in some ways a very sophisticated, intellectual church. Its members were the type who wanted proof; they wanted something to stimulate their intellectual appetites. But Paul told them that 'since in the wisdom of God the world through its wisdom did not know him, God was pleased through the foolishness of what was preached to save those who believe' (1 Cor. 1:21).

Now you may think this is foolishness, and we agree; God might have done it a different way, but he chose to do it *this* way, and the only way you will ever be saved is by faith. Something happens inside. Yet some day everyone will see who Jesus is. Revelation 1:7 describes what will happen when Jesus returns to earth:

> Look, he is coming with the clouds, and every eye will see him, even those who pierced him; and all the peoples of the earth will mourn because of him.

John went on to describe the same event in a different way:

> Then the kings of the earth, the princes, the generals, the rich, the mighty, and every slave and every free man hid in caves and among the rocks of the mountains. They called to the mountains and the rocks, 'Fall on us and hide us from the face of him who sits on the throne and from the wrath of the Lamb! For the great day of their wrath has come, and who can stand?' (Rev. 6:15–17).

Remember, entering the kingdom of God is by invitation alone, for only the sovereign has the right to determine who enters his presence. Hebrews 4:16 says: 'Let us then approach the throne of grace with confidence, so that we may receive mercy and find grace to help us in our time of need.' Here is the invitation sinful people need: King Jesus invites them to enter his presence and approach his throne with confidence.

There is another thing I need to add: this King has come to rule; he demands your utter submission. You cannot have the benefit of his shed blood to cover all your sins unless you become his property. Paul tells us, 'You were bought at a price' (1 Cor. 7:23). Jesus is King, and he asks you to bow before him and surrender everything.

20

The Self-consciousness of Jesus

Revelation 1:10–20

As we have already seen, there are two ways of looking at things: one is to use the analogy of nature, and the other is to use the analogy of faith. If we look at the question 'Who is Jesus?' and try to answer it at the level of our natural understanding, then we will only see a physical man. But the extraordinary description of Jesus in Revelation 1 immediately confuses anybody who tries to understand it on a natural level, and consequently we are forced to use the analogy of faith. We have to get beyond the physical and see Jesus as the Holy Spirit intends us to see him. What we see then is the true Jesus.

The description of Jesus Christ is so complete that the absence of any part of the description would invalidate the others because every part of the description fits together perfectly. For example, if Christ is not inseparably joined to his church, then he could never be the head and centre of it; if Jesus Christ is not the embodiment of the Mosaic law, as the description clearly shows, then the church would have no continuity with the Old Testament Israel, and the title that Jesus used, 'Son of Man' has no biblical significance at all. Furthermore, if Christ is not the promised Messiah of the Old Testament, then he would bear no relationship to the God of the Old Testament, in which case we would have to consider the Christ of the New Testament a fraud and that the Messiah has not yet come. The description of Jesus tells us, 'His head and hair were white like wool, as white as snow' (Rev. 1:14). Now, without this, we would be robbed of the understanding of the person of Jesus that is vital to his very being, for it is an obvious reference to his age and to his mind.

What *kind* of mind did Jesus have? Men and women consist of body and soul. Here, the soul of Jesus is described. The soul consists of intellect and will, and to understand the mind of Jesus we must understand this. I will try to show you why this is important. It is not our concern to know how Jesus looked, the shape of his face, the colour of his skin, or the size of his body; instead, we want to know who he was, what he did and what he said. Moreover, we need to know something of his character, his conduct, how he thought and, especially, how he regarded himself. As we have already seen, the apostle Paul described Jesus as 'the last Adam' (1 Cor. 15:45). Jesus did what the first Adam did *not* do: he obeyed God's will perfectly; or to put it conversely, Jesus, the last (or second) Adam, did *not* do what the first Adam did: he did not sin. This did not lessen his humanity, but accentuated it. Jesus, the true man, showed us what God intended men and women to be.

But there is yet another difference between the second Adam and the first Adam. The latter was created a mature man, whereas Jesus, the second Adam, was *born*. As a child, he developed physically, mentally and emotionally until he reached adulthood.

The question of Jesus' intellect fascinates many, and indeed some think it is supremely important. But all they want to consider when they think of the mind of Jesus is his intelligence, and this is something that can be grasped at the level of natural understanding. I will not pause here for long, except to make one or two important observations.

When Jesus was twelve years old, the Bible tells us that Mary and Joseph took him to Jerusalem for the Feast of the Passover. After it was over they began their return journey, thinking that Jesus was with them. They had travelled some distance before they realized that he was missing and that they would have to retrace their steps to look for him. In fact, they had to go all the way back to Jerusalem, where they discovered Jesus in the temple, fascinating the Rabbis with his knowledge of theology. 'Everyone who heard him was amazed at his understanding and his answers' (Luke 2:47). So even as a child, Jesus displayed great intellect, and Luke tells us that 'Jesus grew in wisdom and stature, and in favour with God and men' (Luke 2:52).

Many people see Jesus as one who was very wise: he knew precisely how to move a crowd; he was a great preacher, an orator and an excellent teacher. Matthew's gospel says that when he finished the Sermon on the Mount, 'The crowds were amazed at his teaching, because he taught as one who had authority, and not as their teachers of the law' (Matt. 7:28–29). Furthermore, in Matthew 13:54-56 we read this:

> Coming to his home town, he began teaching the people in their synagogue, and they were amazed. 'Where did this man get this wisdom, and these miraculous powers?' they asked. 'Isn't this the carpenter's son? Isn't his mother's name Mary, and aren't his brothers, James, Joseph, Simon, and Judas? Aren't all his sisters with us? Where then did this man get all these things?'

This interesting comment shows that these people were surprised that he could speak like that; they knew him because he came from their neighbourhood. Nothing about his appearance arrested their attention; what fascinated them was his wisdom.

Then there was the time when the Pharisees came, determined to trap Jesus by asking whether it was right to pay taxes to Caesar:

> But Jesus, knowing their evil intent, said, 'You hypocrites, why are you trying to trap me? Show me the coin used for paying the tax.' They brought him a denarius, and he asked them, 'Whose portrait is this? And whose inscription?'
>
> 'Caesar's,' they replied.
>
> Then he said to them, 'Give to Caesar what is Caesar's, and to God what is God's.'
>
> When they heard this, they were amazed. So they left him and went away (Matt. 22:18–22).

We read that on another occasion the chief priests and Pharisees asked the temple guards why they had not arrested Jesus, and the guards replied, 'No-one ever spoke the way this man does' (John 7:46).

However, all that I have said so far can be understood with our natural minds, whether or not we are Christians. Seeing Jesus merely as a child prodigy, an intelligent man, as a great speaker or as one who is very shrewd and could deal with his critics, is to use the analogy of nature, and if that is all you see in Jesus, you will miss seeing who he really is. To grasp that, you must take him seriously when he himself tells us what he came to do. John 5 helps us see how Jesus saw himself and to understand his mind.

The mind of Christ, of course, does not refer only to his intelligence, to his shrewdness, to his ability to sway a crowd, it refers to his inner man, to the quality of his soul and his own self-consciousness. In this chapter of John's gospel we see Jesus as one who came to *do* God's will, as one who claimed to *know* God's will, and then as one who claimed to *carry out* God's will.

Now it is one thing to say we intend to do God's will; it is still another to say we know what God's will is, but the crucial thing is, whether having known it, we carry it out. Many of us stumble at the second point: knowing God's will. This is one of the first issues that confronts new Christians and continues to challenge them throughout life. I have been a Christian for many years, but I must confess that at times I am not sure I am much closer really to knowing God's will now than I was a week after I was converted.

Yet the extraordinary thing is, Jesus said, 'My food is to do the will of him who sent me and to finish his work' (John 4:34). So not only did Jesus claim that he came to do God's will, but he claimed to know God's will, but the most extraordinary thing of all is that he carried it out.

Jesus said, 'My Father is always at his work to this very day, and I, too, am working' (John 5:17).

Now if you have recently become a Christian and say you are certain that you know what God wants you to do tomorrow and thereafter, that you know his will perfectly, be warned: that is a very dangerous claim, for that statement immediately put Jesus equal with God. Only Jesus could say that. If you still do not realize the significance of saying that, all you have to do is read the next verse, and see the reaction of the Jews: 'For this reason the Jews tried all the harder to kill him; not only was he breaking the Sabbath, but he was even calling God his own Father, making himself equal with God' (v. 18).

Jesus' reply to the Jews is interesting: 'I tell you the truth, the Son can do nothing by himself' (v. 19). This is perhaps the most explicit admission of his true and full humanity than any other sentence he ever uttered. This is why Jesus had to live by faith; but faith is knowledge and the knowledge must be the knowledge of God's will. Jesus claimed to know God's will, for in the same verse he continued, 'He can do only what he sees his Father doing, because whatever the Father does, the Son also does.'

Jesus also made himself equal to the Father in verse 21: 'For just as the Father raises the dead and gives them life, even so the Son gives life to whom he is pleased to give it.' This means that in the same way that God, the Father Almighty, has the power to raise a person from the dead, so Jesus also has the power to give life to those who are dead in their sins.

Let me explain this: I said earlier that we were going to leave the level of our natural understanding and ascend to the level of faith, and if you understand what I am saying, it means that you too are now operating at the level of faith. Here is another way of putting it: at the level of our natural understanding, the Bible says we are dead, and the ability to grasp spiritual things is something beyond us. What makes the difference, so we can grasp the spiritual, is that Jesus himself has made us alive. Consequently, if you suddenly find yourself perceiving the things that the 'natural' man cannot see, it is the glorious indication that you have been quickened and have been enabled to think at the level of faith. It can only happen to one who has been given life by Christ himself.

Jesus went on to say, 'The Father judges no-one, but has entrusted all judgment to the Son' (v. 22). So we see that Jesus has all authority in heaven and in earth. Furthermore, Jesus himself has the power to give everlasting life, for in verse 24 we read this: 'I tell you the truth, whoever hears my word and believes him who sent me has eternal life.' In other words, if until now you have believed what I have been telling you about Jesus, if you have understood and believed that he came to do God's will, and that he did it, then the promise is yours: you will not be condemned but have 'passed from death to life' (1 John 3:14).

There is one more thing that I want you to see. It is one thing to understand the mind of Christ in the light of the way that he looked at himself, but how did the Father look at Jesus? To put it another way, Jesus *said* he came to do the Father's will; the question is, *did* he? I want us to look at three events in Jesus' life that show he did indeed have his Father's approval.

First there is the occasion of Jesus' baptism. Jesus asked John the Baptist to baptize him. Matthew's gospel says:

> As soon as Jesus was baptised, he went up out of the water. At that moment heaven was opened, and he saw the Spirit of God descending like a dove and lighting on him. And a voice from heaven said, 'This is my Son, whom I love; with him I am well pleased' (Matt. 3:16-17).

So Jesus, who was around thirty years old then, knew that up to that time he had his Father's approval.

The second time his Father showed his approval of his Son happened during Jesus' ministry. Jesus took Peter, James and John up to a high mountain and was transfigured before them. Mark tells us, 'A voice came from the clouds: "This is my Son, whom I love. Listen to him!"' (Mark 9:7). This was confirmation that Jesus had continued to do his Father's will.

The third instance came at the moment Jesus died at Calvary. Now Jesus had claimed that he was going to do the Father's will, and just hours before he was crucified Jesus prayed in the Garden of Gethsemane at the foot of the Mount of Olives. He said, 'My Father, if it is possible, may this cup be taken from me. Yet not as I will, but as you will' (Matt.

26:39). So we see him continuing to carry out his Father's will. The result was that they nailed Jesus to a cross.

Many things happened while he was hanging there, but something happened that was unexpected, even by Jesus himself, for until then he had enjoyed unbroken fellowship with his Father. After Jesus said, 'Father, forgive them, for they do not know what they are doing' (Luke 23:34), and after forgiving the thief on the cross, saying, 'Today you will be with me in paradise' (v. 43) we read that an eerie darkness came over the land, and there was silence, until suddenly, Jesus cried out in Aramaic *'Eloi, Eloi, lama sabachthani?'* (Matt. 27:46). People standing near, not understanding exactly what he was saying, said, 'He's calling Elijah. . . . Let's see if Elijah comes to save him' (vv. 47, 49). But the words were, 'My God, my God, why have you forsaken me?'

It was the only time Jesus ever called the Father *God*. Previously, he had always called him Father. It was a moment Jesus had not anticipated. Had he done something wrong? Had he failed? Had he turned his Father against him? What did this mean? Then, just before he bowed his head and died, he uttered these words, 'It is finished' (John 19:30). The only sign that could be seen or understood then was given several hundred yards away inside the Western Wall of the temple, when the veil of the temple was torn from top to bottom (Matt. 27:51). It was there God put his final affirmation upon all that Jesus had done. He had done his Father's will perfectly, all the way to the cross.

Now you may wonder why Jesus cried out, 'My God, my God, why have you forsaken me?' That was the moment when all our sins were put upon Jesus; that was when he who knew no sin was made sin (2 Cor. 5:21). In that moment he legally became the world's greatest sinner. It was on that cross Jesus did the final thing God asked and took all our sins so that we bear them no more.

In a few sentences Paul sums up everything that Jesus came to do, and which he did:

> Let this mind be in you, which was also in Christ Jesus: Who, being in the form of God, thought it not robbery to be equal with God: But made himself of no reputation, and took upon him the form of a servant, and was made in the likeness of men: And being found in fashion as a man, he humbled himself, and became obedient unto death, even the death of the cross (Phil. 2:5-8, AV).

That is the mind of Christ.

21

Christ Our Wisdom and Righteousness

Revelation 1:14

What did Jesus look like? Many years ago I remember visiting a black church in Nashville, Tennessee. I noticed that behind the baptistery was a mural of Jesus being baptized by John the Baptist, and I saw that both Jesus and John the Baptist were black. Now some say, 'Well, Jesus might have been black, or perhaps he had an Asian or Middle Eastern appearance.' But the description of Jesus in Revelation 1 is given in such a way that you can see his actual facial appearance is irrelevant. For example, John describes a man whose head and hair were 'white like wool, as white as snow' (Rev. 1:14). Surely not! Jesus died at the age of thirty-three, so it is unlikely that such a young man would have had white hair. Yet that is how John describes him. But this description clearly shows that Jesus' appearance is not important. John's vision depicts Jesus in such a way that we are not even to consider him at the level of human understanding. Let me put it this way: not only are pictures of Jesus purely speculative, but even if we had a photograph of Jesus it would not help. As we have seen, if we are to understand who Jesus is, we must understand him at the level of the Holy Spirit.

This description of Jesus' head and his hair gives us three truths: (1) his agelessness and the timeless impact that he made on the world, (2) his purity of mind, and (3) the transparency of his character. Now you may ask why these things are important and you may say, 'I simply want to know what Jesus was like as a man.' But I would do you no favour to present Jesus to you at the level of human understanding. Let me try to explain why.

Jesus himself taught that he was not always going to be on this earth. He told his disciples, 'It is for your good that I am going away. Unless I go away, the Counsellor [the Holy Spirit] will not come to you' (John 16:7). Jesus taught that the Holy Spirit must come, and that he would reveal Jesus at a level beyond natural understanding. Now this is very important, because if you fail to understand this, you will fail to understand what Christianity is about. Do you realize that if the Holy Spirit had not come on the Day of Pentecost Christianity would have never come into being? Do you realize that even the resurrection of Jesus from the dead did not persuade those who saw him to preach the gospel and start the church?

Peter made a very revealing statement after the resurrection. He said, 'I'm going out to fish' (John 21:3). Why do you think Peter said that? After all, he had walked with Jesus for three years, he had been present at every sermon Jesus preached, and, possibly, he had witnessed every miracle Jesus performed. Peter was there when Jesus was transfigured on a high mountain. To cap it all, Peter had seen the risen Saviour. Yet when Jesus disappeared, Peter did not know what to do. So he announced his intention of going fishing. He might have continued to do that for the rest of his life had it not been for the Day of Pentecost.

What brought Christianity into being was, on that day, the Holy Spirit came down from heaven and descended on the disciples. Filled with the Spirit, they clearly saw things that they had never understood before. Their minds grasped everything concerning the Messiah as he was portrayed in the Old Testament; they saw why Jesus died on the cross, the truth of the resurrection, and they understood their mission in the world.

Now the tragedy is that we have largely forgotten these things in the twentieth century. Although what I am about to describe had its roots hundreds of years earlier, in the nineteenth century Germany witnessed a phenomenon that spread throughout the Christian world and became known as 'nineteenth century liberalism'. For years it was also called 'modernism'. Those who were modernists did not mind the term, and those who were not used it pejoratively to condemn those who held that viewpoint.

There was a wave of feeling that we need to return to the *man* Jesus – seemingly, an innocent pursuit; they called it 'the quest for the historical Jesus'. A thesis was put forward that it was a man by the name of Saul of Tarsus who 'muddied the waters', and were it not for the apostle Paul, as he became known, Christianity would have been altogether different. 'What a pity,' many scholars thought, 'that Christianity has been coloured by Paul's theology.' So the quest for the historical Jesus was one that tried to separate the life of Jesus from the 'evil' influence of Paul.

Theology in some places was never the same again, and although we call it 'nineteenth century liberalism', it is still around today. Contemporary interest in the question 'Who is Jesus?' still reveals the remnants of that theology in television documentaries, musicals and Hollywood films. These try to portray Jesus at the level of human understanding and bring you no closer to knowing him. Yet even if modern technology existed two thousand years ago and you had Jesus' photograph, even if they had televised Jesus preaching the Sermon on the Mount or filmed the crucifixion and the empty tomb, these things too would bring you no closer to knowing him. But the sad fact is that many people think that is the way to understand Jesus, who he was and what he did. There is still the view that we need to forget Paul. Put him aside and let us get back to Jesus. That is the idea.

Jesus said it was expedient for his followers that he went away because it was necessary for the Holy Spirit to come down to reveal who he was and why he came. If we leave the Holy Spirit aside, our knowledge of Jesus is confined to the level of human understanding. This is why the Jews in that era hated Paul, and it explains why many people hate him to this very day: Paul refused to consider Jesus at the natural level. Let me quote something Paul said about this: 'So from now on we regard no-one from a worldly point of view. Though we once regarded Christ in this way, we do so no longer' (2 Cor. 5:16). Regarding Jesus on a natural level offends no one, but here is the offence of Christianity: Paul said that we can only truly understand the person of Jesus at the level of the Holy Spirit.

The Holy Spirit ordains that one way in which Jesus is to be made known is through preaching. You may think that this is foolish, and Paul would be the first to agree with you. He called it 'foolishness'.

> It pleased God by the foolishness of preaching to save them that believe. For the Jews require a sign, and the Greeks seek after wisdom: But we preach Christ crucified, unto the Jews a stumblingblock, and unto the Greeks foolishness; But unto them which are called, both Jews and Greeks, Christ the power of God, and the wisdom of God (1 Cor. 1:21–24, AV).

When Jesus Christ is preached, some will love him, some will hate him, some will see him as 'foolishness', some will see him as 'a stumblingblock', but others will see him as 'the power of God'. A Christian is not one who can answer the question 'Who is Jesus?' on the natural level, but one who has seen in Jesus what Paul saw when he said, 'So from now on we regard no-one from a worldly point of view. Though we once regarded Christ in this way, we do so no longer' (2 Cor. 5:16).

Some think that if they could only study archaeology and find proof that Jesus existed, or go to Gethsemane and find the very rock that he knelt beside, or walk down the streets that he walked on and make a pilgrimage to the place of the crucifixion, and so forth, it would make all the difference and they would feel they really knew him. But you don't need to go to Israel, you can come to know Jesus in the place where you are. We can share the same knowledge that his disciples had. Jesus is not limited to one little sphere, to one place on the map or to one date in history. Hundreds of years earlier Daniel had a vision that was similar to the one John had. He saw this Son of Man, whose hair was 'white like wool, as white as snow', and he called him 'the Ancient of Days' (Dan. 7:9). Jesus is not limited by geography nor is he limited by time. This is what I mean about the agelessness of the person of Jesus.

To become a Christian is to see Jesus not only at the natural level but also at the *super*natural level. We can all find in Jesus 'the power of God and the wisdom of God'. It has nothing to do with IQ, it has nothing to do with our educational background, nor does it depend on whether we have been brought up in Christian homes or whether we have been churchgoers. What makes the difference is when the Holy Spirit takes hold of us, the same Spirit who came down on the Day of Pentecost, and for the first time we see the *real* Jesus.

Let us look again at what Paul said in 1 Corinthians 1:21-24 (AV):

It pleased God by the foolishness of preaching to save them that believe. For the Jews require a sign, and the Greeks seek after wisdom: But we preach Christ crucified, unto the Jews a stumblingblock, and unto the Greeks foolishness; But unto them which are *called*, both Jews and Greeks, Christ the power of God, and the wisdom of God.

You may want to know what that calling is. The Bible tells us that it is a twofold calling: (1) there is the calling at the natural level when you hear and remember the gospel message and (2) the calling when the Holy Spirit reveals Jesus and something happens inside you.

Sometimes we may wonder why God called *us*; most of us are ordinary people, neither rich, influential nor famous. But Paul pointed out that those who are called are generally not from the upper classes, or even from the middle classes. In 1 Corinthians 1:26-27 he put it this way:

Brothers, think of what you were when you were called. Not many of you were wise by human standards; not many were influential; not many were of noble birth. But God chose the foolish things of the world to shame the wise.

God chose the base things of the world, the things that people despise. Do you know why? So no one would glory in his presence. God is not interested in flattering our intellects. Far from it, when we decide to become Christians, it is because we recognize that in the sight of God we are a heinous sight. Paul dared to reveal the truth and this is why he was (and still is in certain circles) unpopular. Yet you can see how Paul's thinking is coherent with John's vision, for John was also looking at Jesus at the level of the Holy Spirit.

Now we need to look at the purity of Jesus' mind. Our

minds are not pure: we have evil thoughts of greed, lust, envy, jealousy, hate and vengeance. God hates sin. Moreover, he requires that we know his will perfectly. None of *us* do. Yet one man did, one whose mind was pure. Although Jesus was tempted, he did not succumb to evil thoughts.

The wonderful thing that happens to those of us who become Christians is that the wisdom of Jesus, his pure mind and his perfect apprehension of God's will are imputed to us. That means that his perfection is credited to our account. Now this is very important. I take great comfort in this, because none of us know God's will perfectly. However, Jesus had perfect wisdom and purity of mind. That is why we need him as our Saviour

John said, 'In the beginning was the Word [Jesus], and the Word was with God, and the Word was God' (John 1:1). Jesus did not have his beginning in Bethlehem, for Jesus has always existed, and not only is he with God, he *is* God. Galatians 4:4-5 tells us, 'When the time had fully come, God sent his Son, born of a woman, born under law, to redeem those under law, that we might receive the full rights of sons.' Jesus made-a-once-for-all appearance, and his life culminated in his death on a Roman cross, and what Jesus did on the cross was sufficient for ever. 'What did he do?' you may ask. The Bible tells us, 'He did not enter by means of the blood of goats and calves; but he entered the Most Holy Place once for all by his own blood, having obtained eternal redemption' (Heb. 9:12).

The next thing that I want to show you is found in Hebrews 10:10: 'We have been made holy through the sacrifice of the body of Jesus Christ once for all.' And Hebrews 10:12 says, 'When this priest had offered for all time one sacrifice for sins, he sat down at the right hand of God.' My point is this: his head and his hairs were 'white like wool, as white as snow' showing his eternality, and when he came to this world, what he did on the cross he did *once* and that was enough for all time.

The final thing I want you to understand is Jesus' righteousness, which encompasses the way he lived as well as his death. Some have taught that what he did between Good Friday and Easter Sunday is all that matters. Theologians sometimes call this the 'passive obedience' of Jesus, but you also need to know that there is what we call the 'active obedience' of Jesus that extended throughout his life. God has given us his moral law – the Ten Commandments. You and I break God's law every day in thought, in word, and sometimes in deed. While he lived, Jesus kept that law perfectly. The Bible tells us that this man that John saw in a vision, whose 'head and hair were white like wool, as white as snow', was perfectly righteous.

'Why is that important?' you may ask. Because it means that our feelings of failure and guilt can be wiped away. Many years before Jesus came, the prophet Isaiah said: '"Come now, let us reason together," says the Lord. "Though your sins are like scarlet, they shall be as white as snow; though they are red as crimson, they shall be like wool"' (Isa. 1:18). No matter how guilty we may be, Jesus, whose 'head and his hair were white like wool, as white as snow', whose pure mind, whose righteousness is imputed to us, will take away that guilt and we may be washed clean and know that 'as far as the east is from the west' is how far he has removed our sins from us (Ps. 103:12).

Therefore Paul summed it all up in these words:

'It is because of him that you are in Christ Jesus, who has become for us wisdom from God – that is, our righteousness, holiness and redemption (1 Cor. 1:30).

22

The Wrath of the Lamb (Part 1)

Revelation 1:14

We come now to that part of John's depiction of Jesus in Revelation 1 that has been the most neglected and the least understood. John says, 'His eyes were like blazing fire' (v. 14).

On the eve of his crucifixion, Jesus prayed, 'Father, glorify me in your presence with the glory I had with you before the world began' (John 17:5). In John's vision we see that God has indeed restored Jesus to his former glory. Moreover, we see now that Jesus, whose 'eyes were like blazing fire', is all that God is, in his wrath, in his justice and in his holiness.

When Jesus was on earth, he was portrayed as the Lamb of God. You may remember that John the Baptist proclaimed him as 'the Lamb of God, who takes away the sin of the world' (John 1:29). The prophet Isaiah also depicted Jesus as a lamb. Foreseeing the Messiah several hundred years before Jesus' birth, Isaiah said, 'He was oppressed and afflicted, yet he did not open his mouth; he was led like a lamb to the slaughter, and as a sheep before her shearers is silent, so he did not open his mouth' (Isa. 53:7).

An interesting story in Acts 8:26–39 tells how Philip, one of the original seven deacons, came upon a man from Ethiopia, who was reading that very passage from Isaiah. The Holy Spirit said to Philip, 'Go and talk to that man.' So Philip approached the Ethiopian and, seeing what he was reading, asked, 'Do you understand that passage of Scripture?' The Ethiopian answered, 'How can I unless someone explains it to me?' Then Philip explained that it described Jesus, the Lamb of God.

Yet in Revelation 1 the same Lamb of God, who is himself God, takes on that very facet of the divine nature that his earthly life tended to disguise: he is revealed as a God of justice. In the Bible, particularly throughout the Old Testament, there is no clearer teaching than that of God's justice in punishing sin. The God of the Old Testament is repeatedly revealed as a God of wrath. Then Jesus, the Lamb of God, came to the earth. He offered mercy and forgiveness to the repentant sinner, he showed compassion for the broken-hearted, he healed the sick, he cast out demons and raised the dead. Jesus seemed to disguise the wrath and justice of God. But John also describes Jesus with eyes 'like blazing fire', and we see that the Lamb of God is not only the embodiment of God's mercy, but, having been absorbed in the totality of the divine being and attributes, he is also the embodiment of God's wrath.

Revelation 6 speaks of the terror unconverted men and women will experience when Jesus returns and they contemplate God's anger:

I watched as he opened the sixth seal. There was a great earthquake. The sun turned black like sackcloth made of goat hair, the whole moon turned blood red, and the stars in the sky fell to earth, as late figs drop from a fig tree when shaken by a strong wind. The sky receded like a scroll, rolling up, and every mountain and island was removed from its place.

Then the kings of the earth, the princes, the generals, the rich, the mighty, and every slave and every free man hid in caves and among the rocks of the mountains. They called to the mountains and the rocks, 'Fall on us and hide us from the face of him who sits on the throne and from the wrath of the Lamb. For the great day of their wrath has come, and who can stand?' (Rev. 6:12–17).

Jesus the Saviour will return as Jesus the Judge. The same Lamb of God that now takes away sin will come to punish it. It is *this* Jesus John saw in his vision, one whose eyes 'were like a blazing fire'.

However, the New Testament says that judgment must 'begin with the family of God' (1 Pet. 4:17). This means that because Christ is present in his church and holds the churches and its ministers in his hand, he is determined that the church, which is his body, is holy, as he intended it to be. So judgment begins with the church.

Let us examine this for a moment. It is interesting that when Jesus addressed the various churches in Asia, his description in Revelation 1 was broken down and one or two parts of it were given to each church, corresponding to the condition of that church. Let us look at four examples demonstrating this.

First, consider the beginning of Jesus' message to the church at Ephesus. Jesus said, 'To the angel of the church in Ephesus write [these things]'. We see that the letter begins with a description of Jesus similar to John's depiction of Jesus in Revelation 1, but not giving the total picture, just a part of it. 'These are the words of him who holds the seven stars in his right hand and walks among the seven golden lampstands' (Rev. 2:1). Then, after Jesus spoke about the condition of that church, he said: 'Remember the height from which you have fallen! Repent and do the things you did at first. If you do not repent, I will come to you and remove your lampstand from its place' (Rev. 2:5). Here we find the warning correlated with that description. Second, consider the letter to the church at Smyrna. The description begins, 'These are the words of him who is the First and the Last, who died and came to life again' (Rev. 2:8). We see that this church at Smyrna, receiving no condemnation, was simply given the promise in verse 11, 'He who overcomes will not be hurt at all by the second death.'

The third example I take concerns the church at Pergamum; Jesus described himself as he 'who has the sharp double-edged sword' (Rev. 2:12). But when the condemnation had been given, this warning followed: 'Repent therefore! Otherwise, I will soon come to you and will fight against them with the sword of my mouth' (Rev. 2:16).

Now we come to my fourth example, the letter to the church at Thyatira; here, the description drawn from Revelation 1 is this: 'These are the words of the Son of God, whose eyes are like blazing fire and whose feet are like burnished bronze' (Rev. 2:18). Why was such a description given to this church? The answer is that judgment must begin with the family of God. Jesus said, 'You tolerate that woman Jezebel, who calls herself a prophetess. By her teaching she misleads my servants into sexual immorality and the eating of food sacrificed to idols' (Rev. 2:20). He looked at this church with 'eyes like blazing fire' because he was angry that a church should be in that condition. This church had turned God's grace into lasciviousness; it had become a playhouse, a church where God's people were unrecognizable, a church whose ministers were teaching the very opposite of the gospel, and who were propagating lies and encouraging men and women to sin and to live ungodly, worldly lives. So Jesus came down to this church with 'eyes like blazing fire', for he will not tolerate such evil behaviour. He went on to say this:

'I have given her time to repent of her immorality, but she is unwilling. So I will cast her on a bed of suffering, and I will make those who commit adultery with her suffer intensely, unless they repent of her ways. I will strike her children dead. Then all the churches will know that I am he who searches hearts and minds, and I will repay each of you according to your deeds' (Rev. 2:21-23).

You see, Jesus is concerned about his witness in the world: he cares about his reputation, and when people who are called by his name turn his grace into ungodliness, his anger is roused. So when judgment comes, it begins with Christians, who are his church. This is why Paul, writing to the Corinthian church said, 'So, if you think you are standing firm, be careful that you don't fall!' (1 Cor. 10:12).

This comes as a warning to anybody thinking about becoming a Christian, because they need to know that if they do, they take Jesus' name. He is jealous of his name, and expects those who bear it to uphold his honour in this world. They need to know the kind of life Jesus expects his people to live because he is determined to deal with those who dishonour his name. Remember that judgment must begin 'with the family of God'.

However, Peter has more to say on the subject of judgment: 'If it begins with us, what will the outcome be for those who do not obey the gospel of God? And if it is hard for the righteous to be saved, what will become of the ungodly and the sinner?' (1 Pet. 4:17–18). Do you wonder why it will be worse for ungodly people, who have never made a profession of faith? I believe there are three reasons.

First, ungodly people, sinners who never profess the name of Christ, do not receive a warning about their behaviour as those who do, because those who become part of God's church join a class of people with whom God shares certain truths. Speaking to the church in Laodicea, Jesus said, 'Those whom I love I rebuke and discipline' (Rev. 3:19). We cannot have Jesus as Saviour without also having him as Lord. He retains the right to govern our lives, and if we go astray he has a way of correcting us. God sometimes deals with us severely. Why does he do it? Because he loves us. As Peter said, judgment begins 'with the family of God' (1 Pet. 4:17). But to those who have never professed the name of Christ, no warning is given.

The second reason that it is worse for those who are not Christians is this: people who never profess faith in Christ live out their lives without the providential restraint of their wickedness. Now in a way that is not *entirely* true, because though they may not be Christians, and though they are wicked, most are not as wicked as they might be. But it is only because of God's general love for humanity that they are not worse than they are. What I mean is, though they are sinners, God allows them to prosper. Now they may take their prosperity as a sign that they are not totally bad, but the fact is, God does not restrain them: he allows them to continue making money, to achieve their ambitions and to enjoy the pleasures this world affords. He lets them go their way without hindrance.

The third reason it will be worse for the unconverted is because the first punishment they will ever know is the undiluted wrath of God upon them eternally. That company of people John describes in Revelation 6:16, who were desperately trying to hide, crying for the rocks to fall on them and hide them will be a company of which they will be a part.

If you are unconverted, you may say, 'Well, I know professing Christians who do bad things. I wouldn't dream of doing some things they do.' You are right, and God is

deeply concerned about their behaviour. This is why I quoted
the verse 'Those whom I love I rebuke and discipline' (Rev.
3:19). Some of God's people do fall into sin, but he
disciplines them for it. Moreover, their chastening is in this
lifetime alone; it is temporal. But God does not discipline
those who are outside his family. The first punishment the
ungodly will experience is when they face Jesus on Judgment
Day. Their punishment is not temporal but eternal.

If you are reading this and you are not yet a Christian,
God has granted you the first fruit of his kindness, because
he has begun to treat you as though you were his, for he has
warned you. There is hope for you still. The Lamb of God,
who is coming to punish sin, offers to forgive you. Jesus
shed his blood that you might become a child of God, a
member of his family, whom he will love, correct and defend.

23

The Wrath of the Lamb (Part 2)

Revelation 1:14–15

You will recall that when Jesus addressed the seven churches in Asia, one or two parts of the description of Jesus in Revelation 1 were given to each church, corresponding to its particular condition. The church at Thyatira was one of the seven churches Jesus selected, and I think everybody would agree that this church was in a worse condition than the other six. This is why Jesus' address to that church begins with those elements of his description from Revelation 1 that symbolize his wrath: 'These are the words of the Son of God, whose eyes are like blazing fire and whose feet are like burnished bronze' (Rev. 2:18).

In the Thyatiran church disgraceful things were taking place. Jesus said:

> 'Nevertheless I have this against you: You tolerate that woman Jezebel, who calls herself a prophetess. By her teaching she misleads my servants into sexual immorality and the eating of food sacrificed to idols. I have given her time to repent of her immorality, but she is unwilling. So I will cast her on a bed of suffering, and I will make those who commit adultery with her suffer intensely, unless they repent of her ways' (Rev. 2:20-22).

It is very sad that people who called themselves Christians could lower themselves to behave like this. Yet it is happening in modern times too. Many cults and sects have sprung up that are centred around sex. Even within evangelicalism there is the danger of antinomianism, where people, under the pretence of grace, excuse their wicked living.

Thyatira was a church that saw no wrong in what it did, and so when Jesus addressed that church he chose to describe himself as one whose eyes are 'like blazing fire' and whose feet are 'like burnished bronze'. Since Jesus himself chose to couple together the descriptions of his eyes and feet we should do the same.

The descriptions of Jesus' eyes and his feet have this in common: both are symbolic of his earthly ministry. So we need to look at the person of Christ in terms of his eyes and his feet as he is depicted in his earthly ministry and then as he is described by John. Now it is possible you have only seen one side of this description, but to understand who Jesus is you need to see the whole picture.

In his earthly ministry the eyes and the feet of Jesus reflect his infinite tenderness, his infinite acceptance and his infinite compassion. This makes a wonderful study and I can only give you a taste of it here.

Let us begin by thinking about Jesus' eyes. Now whenever we see Jesus in terms of what he sees we should note it. For example, in Matthew 5:1–2 we read, 'When he saw the crowds, he went up on a mountainside and sat down. His disciples came to him and he began to teach them.' Then Jesus gave the Sermon on the Mount. He saw the multitude and he wanted to explain the kingdom to them. It began with his eyes.

Let us go a step further, Matthew 8:14-15 says, 'When Jesus came into Peter's house, he saw Peter's mother-in-law lying in bed with a fever. He touched her hand and the fever left her, and she got up and began to wait on him.' Jesus *saw* a need and he immediately responded to it.

Then in Matthew 9:2-3 we read, 'Some men brought to him a paralytic, lying on a mat. When Jesus saw their faith, he said to the paralytic, "Take heart, son; your sins are forgiven."' Jesus saw their faith.

In Matthew 9:20–22 we have the well-known account of the woman who had been haemorrhaging for twelve years. She thought that it was impossible to speak directly to Jesus because of the people thronging around him. However, she believed that if she could only work her way through the crowd and touch the hem of his robe she would be healed. This she did. Sensing that someone had touched him, Jesus turned around. When he saw the woman, he did not reprimand her but gently said, 'Take heart, daughter, your faith has healed you.' Once again, Jesus saw somebody's faith.

In John 11 we have the account of the death of Lazarus. His sisters, Martha and Mary, sent word to Jesus that their brother was ill, but by the time Jesus arrived it was too late and Lazarus was dead. Mary and Martha rebuked Jesus for his delay (vv. 21, 32), and we read that Mary wept.

> When Jesus saw her weeping, and the Jews who had come along with her also weeping, he was deeply moved in spirit and troubled. 'Where have you laid him?' he asked.
> 'Come and see, Lord,' they replied.
> Jesus wept (vv. 33–35).

Jesus saw Mary's tears, and wept with her.

These stories simply give a hint of the eyes of Jesus in his earthly ministry – eyes of acceptance, eyes that shed tears of compassion. Our Lord was one who could weep with those who were in need.

What about his feet? I think we must begin with Isaiah 52:7, a verse that the apostle Paul quoted in Romans 10:15. It says: 'How beautiful on the mountains are the feet of those who bring good news, who proclaim peace; who bring good tidings, who proclaim salvation, who say to Zion "Your God reigns!"' The feet to which this verse refers belong to Jesus.

In the New Testament we read in Luke 4 how Jesus went into the synagogue on the Sabbath day and stood up to read. He opened the book of Isaiah and read these words, which he later applied to himself.

> The Spirit of the Lord is on me,
> because he has anointed me to preach good news to the poor.
> He has sent me to proclaim freedom for the prisoners
> and recovery of sight for the blind,
> to release the oppressed,
> to proclaim the year of the Lord's favour (vv. 18-19).

Why do we have feet? They are, of course, our means of getting around, and there is nothing more wonderful than when someone comes to you with good news. Wherever Jesus went, he did good things: he was always healing the sick, mending broken hearts and giving hope to repentant sinners.

In Luke 7:36–50 we read the account of what happened when a Pharisee invited Jesus to have dinner with him. After he sat down, a well-known prostitute came in with an alabaster box of perfume. We read that 'as she stood behind him at his feet weeping, she began to wet his feet with her tears. Then she wiped them with her hair, kissed them and poured perfume on them' (v. 38). Why would a wicked woman want to do that? Because Jesus was the first man to treat her with dignity. Her experience of men had been that they saw her only as a sex-object, to be used and then cast aside. But Jesus was different. He treated her with dignity, as a person, and so she kissed his feet. This is how Jesus treats us. He does not use us or manipulate us; he treats us with respect, dignity, and gives us hope.

In Luke 24 we read that when Jesus rose from the dead and appeared to his heartbroken disciples, they could not really believe that it was indeed Jesus they saw. We read:

> Jesus himself stood among them and said to them 'Peace be with you.' They were startled and frightened, thinking they saw a ghost. He said to them, 'Why are you troubled, and why do doubts rise in your minds? Look at my hands and my feet. It is I myself! Touch me and see; a ghost does not have flesh and bones, as you see I have.' When he had said this, he showed them his hands and feet (vv. 36-40).

How beautiful were those feet! They carried Jesus wherever there was a need, and each time he responded, giving words of hope and life, giving dignity and purpose.

However, now I must show you something else: an aspect of the person of Jesus that has largely been hidden from this generation. Jesus' eyes and feet depicted by his earthly ministry symbolize infinite acceptance and compassion, but this is only part of the picture. What John saw in his vision is a portrait of Jesus with eyes that show infinite wrath and relentless justice. In fact, so opposite are these two descriptions that it is staggering to think they describe the same person. John says, 'His eyes were like blazing fire. His feet were like bronze, glowing in a furnace' (Rev. 1:14-15).

John's description of Jesus' feet being 'like bronze glowing in a furnace' means that God's judgment, referred to repeatedly in the Bible, is not an afterthought; God's decree to punish sin was meticulously planned. That judgment will take place in such a way that everyone will know that they had a fair trial. As it says in Genesis 18:25, 'Will not the Judge of all the earth do right?' Those people whom God will send into everlasting punishment for their sins will know that they are receiving *their* just deserts, and they who are told they can enter the eternal city will know that they are also receiving *their* just deserts – not because of their good works, but because they have trusted in Jesus' blood that was shed on the cross.

When Jesus comes a second time, he will come in judgment. On that day his feet, once called 'beautiful' because they brought good news, and his eyes that still regard us with compassion, will be feared by unbelievers. For there will be a relentless judgment, as infinite as is the mercy contained in the good news. But, thank God, we are still on this happy side of that eternal day. The good news now is that there is still hope if you look at him who died on the cross. God forbid that someday, unsaved, you face him who has 'eyes like blazing fire', and 'feet like bronze glowing in a furnace'.

24

The Voice of Jesus

Revelation 1:15

When we attach someone's voice to a person, a particular image immediately comes to mind. If I referred to the voice of Caruso, for instance, you would immediately think of a tenor, perhaps the greatest tenor that ever lived. Or if I were to mention the voice of Winston Churchill, the older generation would immediately think of the voice they used to hear on the radio, especially during the war.

Have you ever wondered what kind of voice Jesus had? Did he have a high voice, a low voice or one that carried for miles so people could hear what he said? The only way of knowing what the voice of Jesus was like would be to get a description from someone who had heard him speaking when he lived on earth. Yet if we expect to learn the answer to the question in this way, we will be disappointed, for the gospels are silent about this and John simply says that his voice was like 'the sound of many waters' (Rev. 1:15, AV). This description of Jesus' voice is most disappointing to someone who wants to know what Jesus really sounded like. But we have seen that John's description of Jesus defies human understanding. We can only understand the person of Jesus at the level of the Holy Spirit.

Yet why did John compare Jesus' voice to 'the sound of many waters'? I think the answer is simple and obvious: water can produce many sounds, depending on external conditions; similarly, the voice of Jesus is heard in many ways, depending on the conditions that confront him. Although you could doubtless think of more, I want to put before you five ways in which the varying sounds of water describe the voice of Jesus.

First, let us think of the roar of a waterfall cascading from a great height – the voice of power and authority. The best-known sermon that Jesus ever preached we all know as the Sermon on the Mount. When he finished that sermon, the immediate reaction of all who heard it was this: 'He taught as one who had authority, and not as their teachers of the law' (Matt. 7:28-29). In fact, the Bible tells us that the crowds who heard him were 'amazed at his teaching'. We can well understand their surprise, because, in making a series of statements, Jesus took issue with the popular tradition, and this is something that never fails to cause astonishment. For example, Jesus said:

> You have heard that it was said to the people long ago, 'Do not murder, and anyone who murders will be subject to judgment.' But I tell you that anyone who is angry with his brother will be subject to judgment. Again, anyone who says to his brother 'Raca,' is answerable to the Sanhedrin. But anyone who says, 'You fool!' will be in danger of the fire of hell.

> You have heard that it was said, 'Do not commit adultery.' But I tell you that anyone who looks at a woman lustfully has already committed adultery with her in his heart. If your right eye causes you to sin, gouge it out and throw it away. It is better for you to lose one part of your body than for your whole body to be thrown into hell' (Matt. 5:21-22, 27-29).

Jesus went on to say this:

> You have heard that it was said, 'Love your neighbour and hate your enemy.' But I tell you: Love your enemies and pray for those who persecute you, that you may be sons of your Father in heaven (Matt. 5:43–45).

It is interesting that many people admire the Sermon on the Mount at the level of their natural understanding and applaud Jesus for these teachings, particularly the last one. Loving one's enemies is a truly commendable ethic, they think. But they do not like the part about hell, and conveniently forget the Sermon on the Mount had more to say about hell than about heaven. However, if we are to see Jesus at the level of the Spirit we have to reckon with the whole of his word, and we must remember that when Jesus neared the end of his sermon he also said this:

> 'Not everyone who says to me, "Lord, Lord," will enter the kingdom of heaven, but only he who does the will of my Father who is in heaven. Many will say to me on that day, "Lord, Lord, did we not prophesy in your name, and in your name drive out demons and perform many miracles?" Then I will tell them plainly, "I never knew you. Away from me, you evildoers!"'
>
> 'Therefore everyone who hears these words of mine and puts them into practice is like a wise man who built his house on the rock. The rain came down, the streams rose, and the winds blew and beat against that house; yet it did not fall, because it had its foundation on the rock. But everyone who hears these words of mine and does not put them into practice is like a foolish man who built his house on sand. The rain came down, the streams rose, and the winds blew and beat against that house, and it fell with a great crash.'
>
> When Jesus had finished saying these things, the crowds were amazed at his teaching, because he taught as one who had *authority* [my italics], and not as their teachers of the law (Matt. 7:21–29).

On another occasion it was said of him, 'No-one ever spoke the way this man does' (John 7:46). Jesus had authority in his voice. It was with this authority that he went around healing people. Immediately after Jesus preached the Sermon on the Mount, a leper came to him and, falling to his knees, said, 'Lord, if you are willing, you can make me clean' (Matt. 8:2). The Bible tells us that 'Jesus reached out his hand and touched the man. "I am willing," he said. "Be clean!" Immediately he was cured of his leprosy' (v. 3). His words had authority.

A few days later the disciples took Jesus out in their boat on the sea of Galilee and he fell asleep. Suddenly a fierce storm blew up and the sea became so rough that the waves threatened to swamp the boat. In panic, the disciples woke Jesus crying, 'Lord, save us! We're going to drown!' Do you know what Jesus did? He rebuked the wind and the waves and at once there was a great calm. What authority! The disciples were overwhelmed. 'What kind of man is this? Even the winds and the waves obey him!' (see Matt. 8:23–27).

Second, let us think of the sound of the water of a gentle, babbling brook – the voice of peace and forgiveness. Jesus said, 'Come to me, all you who are weary and burdened, and I will give you rest' (Matt. 11:28). Does this description fit you? Are you weary and burdened and yet you don't understand why you feel this way? You may say that you feel guilty, depressed or anxious. People often use these psychological terms to describe their feelings. Perhaps that is the best way you know to explain your unrest right now as you wonder what life is all about. Perhaps you are in deep trouble: you may be in a situation nobody else knows about, and you don't know the solution to your problems. Maybe your marriage is on the rocks or you are in danger of losing your home, or your job or your family. Listen: Jesus has a word for you, 'Come to me, and I will give you rest.'

In case you did not understand that, he put it a different way: 'Take my yoke upon you and learn from me' (v. 29). This means that you recognize that your life is in turmoil and you need to submit yourself to Jesus' lordship and control. But receiving that help is not simply a matter of coming to Christ much as you would visit a doctor, who will, perhaps, give you a prescription to see you through a minor passing illness. Here, we are dealing with something far more serious. The root of your problem is sin: rebellion against your Creator by living in a way contrary to the way he ordained. The 'yoke' Jesus speaks of is not to see you through 'a bad patch'; it is for life.

Listen to the voice of peace and tranquillity. Humble yourself; recognize the turmoil you are in and acknowledge the reason – your sinfulness. You are the kind of person Jesus had in mind when he said, 'I have not come to call the righteous, but sinners to repentance' (Luke 5:32). Jesus was the friend of sinners, and he meets you when, in a broken condition, you truly repent. 'A broken and contrite heart, O God, you will not despise' (Ps. 51:17). Come to God as you are and you will find rest and peace.

Third, let us imagine a deep, still lake. The waters are quiet, almost soundless – the voice of assurance. You will find this assurance simply by looking at Jesus, who died on the cross. Perhaps, until now, you have simply considered Jesus at the level of your natural understanding. You saw a good man and admired his teachings and lamented his violent death. Look to Jesus on that cross again and see what was really happening. It was not something you can see with the naked eye. Even had you been present at the crucifixion, you would have missed it. You will only understand when you grasp hold of God's word and an inner voice convinces you that God's word is true. When this happens, the Bible will suddenly come alive and set you on fire as you read, and you will hear Jesus speaking to you. He will reveal to you what really happened at the crucifixion. You will see that Jesus, who lived a sinless life, willingly took the blame for your sins and God punished him instead of you. You will realize that you must stop competing with what Jesus did on the cross, trusting that your own good deeds will save you; you will understand that Jesus did everything for you. And when you turn to him and accept him as your Saviour, you will hear his voice speaking words of assurance and know that you are his.

However, you need to understand that when you become a Christian, you receive Jesus not only as Saviour but also as Lord. Jesus will rule your life from then on. As Lord he has the right to deal with your life in any way he pleases. If you do anything that brings reproach upon his name, he has a way of reminding you that you are his child, and he can be severe. You may remember he said to the church at Laodicea, 'Those whom I love I rebuke and discipline' (Rev. 3:19). As I said in an earlier chapter, this only happens to those who are Christians. It is a sign of God's love. So when you feel his chastening, you remember that it is further assurance that you are truly his own.

Fourth, think of a raging storm at sea – the voice of anger and displeasure, which those who reject Jesus now will hear someday when he returns to be their Judge. Jesus said, 'A time is coming when all who are in their graves will hear his voice and come out – those who have done good will rise to live, and those who have done evil will rise to be condemned' (John 5:28, 29).

Finally, consider the sound of relentless, pitiless rain – the voice of endless sorrow. Jesus referred to what follows the Final Judgment when he said, 'Many will say to me on that day, "Lord, Lord, did we not prophesy in your name, and in your name drive out demons and perform many miracles?" ' (Matt. 7:22). This means that among their number will be preachers, ministers, vicars and bishops, Roman Catholics, Orthodox and Protestants. Along with many of their flock they may present Jesus with long lists of their good deeds, but these will count for nothing if they have not known Jesus as their Saviour and Lord. They will hear a voice of wrath, a voice consigning them to the place of eternal punishment. Jesus said, 'I will tell them plainly, "I never knew you. Away from me, you evildoers!" ' (v.23). Then they will weep (Matt. 8:12; 25:30; Luke 13:28), but their tears will be too late.

That final day has not yet dawned. Today Jesus' voice, which is like 'the sound of many waters', still pleads, 'Come to me, all you who are weary and burdened, and I will give you rest.'

25

God's Double-edged Sword

Revelation 1:16

Perhaps the most striking thing we shall see in our search to find the answer to the question 'Who is Jesus?' is that he takes on the attributes and character of the God of the Old Testament. This is interesting because many people think Jesus came to reveal the *new* face of God. The God of the Old Testament, as everybody knows, is a God who punishes sin. One Methodist bishop in America went as far as to call the God of the Old Testament 'a bully'. However, many other so-called Christian leaders have also wanted to divorce Christianity from the God of the Old Testament.

That he is so often manifested as a God of wrath and justice in that part of the Bible is not disputed. In fact, it is probably the clearest and most obvious thing we see about the God of the Old Testament. For example, in Genesis we read this:

> Then the LORD said, 'My Spirit will not contend with man for ever.' . . . The LORD saw how great man's wickedness on the earth had become, and that every inclination of the thoughts of his heart was only evil all the time. The LORD was grieved that he had made man on the earth, and his heart was filled with pain. So the LORD said, 'I will wipe mankind, whom I have created, from the face of the earth' (Gen. 6:3, 5–7).

And he did just that.

We think that more people were living on the earth in Noah's day than are living on the earth now. Imagine that! Reliable estimates of the world's population in the time of Noah indicate there were three billion people alive on the earth then. Yet God saved only eight people from the Great Flood – Noah's family. Now if you say, 'I don't like a God like that' you are in good company. Finding anybody who would disagree with you would be most unusual, unless by chance you ask someone whose eyes have been opened by the Holy Spirit and who has come to love the God of the Old Testament.

Yet that is not the last time we find God described as a God of wrath and justice. We read in Genesis 19 that the Lord rained burning sulphur on Sodom and Gomorrah. The Bible says, 'Thus he overthrew those cities and the entire plain, including all those living in the cities—and also the vegetation in the land' (v. 25). God destroyed these people with scarcely a trace. The God of the Old Testament did that.

Now you can well understand that some would want to hold to a vestige of what they would term 'Christianity'. Perhaps, because they were raised in a Christian home or they have seen Christianity has some merit, they don't want to dispense with it altogether. So they say, 'Look, we need to understand that Jesus came to reveal a *different* God.' They cannot accept the idea of the God of the Old Testament, who, when he gave Moses instructions about the way the Hebrews were to prepare the first Passover feast, would say:

> 'They are to take some of the blood [of sacrificed lambs] and put it on the sides and tops of the door frames of the houses where they eat the lambs. . . . On that same night I will pass through Egypt and strike down every firstborn—both men and animals—and I will bring judgment on all the gods of Egypt. I am the LORD' (Exod. 12:7, 12).

Yet I could take you through the five books of Moses and through all the other books of the Old Testament too, but you would see they all reveal the same God. So it is not surprising that many people want to give God a new image that makes him more acceptable in the eyes of the world.

You may ask if there is evidence that Jesus came to give God a new face. My answer is that there is not much, and what evidence there is would be based on selecting sayings of Jesus and quoting them out of their context. I know what I am talking about: I have read the books that proponents of this theory have written and I have studied their theology. They get the idea from the Sermon on the Mount. For example, they read that Jesus said, 'You have heard that it was said, "Eye for eye, and tooth for tooth . . ."' (Matt. 5:38), and immediately they say, 'Ah, that is the God of the Old Testament speaking', and they note that Jesus continues like this:

> 'But I tell you, Do not resist an evil person. If someone strikes you on the right cheek, turn to him the other also. And if someone wants to sue you and take your tunic, let him have your cloak as well. If someone forces you to go one mile, go with him two miles. Give to the one who asks you, and do not turn away from the one who wants to borrow from you.

> 'You have heard that it was said, "Love your neighbour and hate your enemy." But I tell you: Love your enemies and pray for those who persecute you' (vv. 39–44).

These people say, 'Now, that is what I believe. I can accept principles like that.' Consequently, they see this as the *new* face of God.

Now, just a few verses before that passage of Scripture, Jesus says this: 'You have heard that it was said, "Do not

commit adultery"' (v. 27). That sounds like the God of the
Old Testament, doesn't it? Jesus continued, 'But I tell you
that anyone who looks at a woman lustfully has already
committed adultery with her in his heart' (v. 28). Jesus did
not stop there: 'If your right eye causes you to sin, gouge it
out and throw it away. It is better for you to lose one part of
your body than for your whole body to be thrown into hell'
(v. 29). That also sounds like the God of the Old Testament.
Here we have Jesus talking about hell! So those who want
to extract from the sayings of Jesus only that which fits their
concept of God are manifestly hypocritical because they only
select what they like and ignore the other things he said.

But you may say, 'Surely, Jesus came to reveal a God of
love?' Yes, he did. But do you know that it was the God of
the Old Testament who sent Jesus into the world? In fact,
not only did God send him here, but Jesus' crucifixion was
the fulfilment of his plan. God took complete responsibility
for his Son's death. Wicked men crucified Jesus and thought
they had killed him. The devil thought *he* did it. But God
said, '*I* did it.' Why? It was because 'God so loved the world
that he gave his one and only Son, that whoever believes in
him shall not perish but have eternal life' (John 3:16).

However, Christians are those who love the God of the
Old Testament, because they are aware of a sense of sin.
Now their sense of sin is limited, but they can see that God
is justified in all that he does. They cannot explain it; they
cannot tell you why bad things happen, for example, why
there are famines in certain parts of the world, why evil
continues or why a plane can fall from the sky, killing
hundreds of people. They are not that clever, but they know
they are sinners and realize that they have grieved a holy
God. They begin in a small measure to see how much God
hates sin, and the more they understand the more they are

amazed that he saves anybody at all, and the greatest wonder of all is that he would save them.

Jesus came to save us from the wrath to come. Exodus 34:7 tells us 'He [God] does not leave the guilty unpunished.' But the wonderful thing is that God has made a way of escape for the sinner – a way consistent with his own justice, so that sin could be punished but the sinner go free. I referred earlier to the death of Jesus and I said God was responsible. I will tell you how: God hates sin and must punish sinners, but Jesus looked at his Father and said, 'Punish me instead.' God did just that, and Jesus paid the penalty for our sin on the cross.

However, there is a condition to our salvation, as we see in John 3:16: 'God so loved the world that he gave his one and only Son, that whoever *believes* [my italics] in him shall not perish but have eternal life.' Martin Luther called this verse 'the Bible in a nutshell', for it sums up the gospel message.

Now we come to that part of the description of Jesus in Revelation 1 that identifies him with the God who will punish those who reject his Son. We will see Jesus as the Judge, the one who, in the end, will have the task of sending unbelievers to hell. John says, 'Out of his mouth came a sharp double-edged sword' (Rev. 1:16). You may ask what this means. Paul tells us in Ephesians 6:17 that 'the sword of the Spirit . . . is the word of God'. As we all know, a sword is a weapon that may be used defensively or offensively; it is a weapon that has a sharp point that can penetrate the body. It is a deadly weapon: its two edges can be used to slash the enemy, inflict severe pain and kill. Christians can use the sword of the Spirit, the word of God, to attack Satan and to defend themselves when he attacks them.

You may also wonder why Jesus is described as one who

has a sharp double-edged sword coming from his mouth? The answer is, because God's words and Jesus' words are the same (we have already seen that Jesus is not only fully man but also fully God), and God's word has already been identified in Scripture as being sharper than any double-edged sword. Hebrews 4:12 says, 'The word of God is living and active. Sharper than any double-edged sword, it penetrates even to dividing soul and spirit, joints and marrow; it judges the thoughts and attitudes of the heart.' And we find that out of the mouth of Jesus comes 'a sharp double-edged sword' that totally identifies him with the God of the Bible. John saw Jesus depicted in a way that leaves no doubt about his authority. Everything Jesus said in his earthly ministry is true. When you read all that Jesus said, you can be completely confident that you are reading the word of God.

Did you notice that Hebrews 4:12 speaks of how the word of God divides? Let us look at it again. 'The word of God is living and active. Sharper than any double-edged sword, it penetrates even to dividing soul and spirit, joints and marrow; it judges the thoughts and attitudes of the heart.' How can the word of God do that? Simply because it is 'living'. It is not dead; it has power and can penetrate your conscience when nothing else will. God's word is so powerful that it can change the most stubborn person. It can turn someone who in the eyes of the world is a complete failure into a success. It can mend a broken heart. God's word can do that because it is powerful; it overcomes all odds.

Moreover, we find that when it penetrates your conscience, it brings out your truest motives and feelings and makes you face the truth about yourself. I recognize that psychologists and psychiatrists have their place and can help disturbed people, but the word of God does what the

most proficient psychiatrist cannot do, and that is to make
you come face to face with how you *really* are. The word of
God penetrates and is 'sharper than any double-edged sword'.
You see, we are dealing here not with a heart surgeon or a
brain surgeon but with the *master* surgeon, who operates on
a person and reaches what others cannot. The wisest
physician cannot find a person's soul; the most brilliant
surgeon cannot find the conscience, but through his word
God does this.

I know what it is to have an operation; I have had both
my gall-bladder and my appendix removed. Interestingly,
when the master surgeon operates and the double-edged
sword pierces your heart and your conscience, instead of
taking something from you to make you well, he reconstructs
you and makes you a whole person. God does what human
surgeons cannot do.

However, if you are thinking of becoming a Christian, I
must warn you that the word of God has another way of
dividing: it may separate you from your dearest friends or
loved ones. In Matthew 10 Jesus says:

'Do not suppose that I have come to bring peace to the earth. I
did not come to bring peace, but a sword. For I have come to
turn

'a man against his father,
a daughter against her mother,
a daughter-in-law against her mother-in-law—
a man's enemies will be the members of his own household.

'Anyone who loves his father and mother more than me is not
worthy of me; anyone who loves his son or daughter more
than me is not worthy of me; and anyone who does not take
his cross and follow me is not worthy of me. Whoever finds

his life will lose it, and whoever loses his life for my sake will find it' (vv. 34–39).

You need to know that if you become a Christian life will never be the same again. The things that you once lived for will lose their appeal, and the things that you once thought that you could never love will become dear to you. You will want to come to church, and you will want to read your Bible; you will want to come to the communion table, and you will want to give of your means to spread the gospel. So your friends and relatives will regard you differently, and your relationship with them will never be the same again. But you will have new relationships now – you will have brothers and sisters in Christ.

Nevertheless, you must recognize that not only will you find yourself part of a new family but you will gain a new enemy, the like of which you have never known – the devil. Satan will be enraged when you become a Christian; Jesus Christ is his arch-enemy, so when you align yourself with Jesus, the devil becomes your enemy too and he will hate you with an infinite hatred.

However, God's double-edged sword is a miraculous weapon. The sword, which is the word of God, becomes your means of defeating the devil. In Ephesians 6:16–17 Paul tells us how to overcome Satan: 'Take up the shield of faith, with which you can extinguish all the flaming arrows of the evil one. Take the helmet of salvation and the sword of the Spirit, which is the word of God.' So you need to know your Bible. A new world awaits you as you read this marvellous book, and the more you know it, the more able you will be in dealing with the enemy of your soul. You begin to see how he shows himself in unexpected ways, and so you are not all that surprised when he attacks you.

Remember, the Bible is a weapon you use defensively and offensively in your Christian life.

God's double-edged sword is a deadly weapon, and when it penetrates your heart, you must die. You must die to your pride and to everything that is dear to you. Jesus said, 'Whoever finds his life will lose it, and whoever loses his life for my sake will find it' (Matt. 10:39). Put your life in the hands of the master surgeon, and he will make you whole and give you eternal life. This doubled-edged sword is indeed a miraculous weapon.

26

The Right Hand of God

Revelation 1:17

We have seen that Revelation 1 describes Jesus in terms of clothing, his voice, his hair, his eyes and his feet, yet if we are to understand the person of Jesus, we cannot complete this study without looking at his hands. Revelation 1 refers to Jesus' right hand twice. First, John says, 'In his right hand he held seven stars' (v.16), and then, 'When I saw him, I fell at his feet as though dead. Then he placed his right hand on me' (v. 17).

Now whereas in previous chapters we have been emphasizing that we need to see Jesus at the level of the Spirit, we must not forget that when he was on earth it was possible to know and see him in a physical sense. In fact, one disciple would not have it any other way. After the resurrection, the disciples told Thomas that Jesus had appeared to them while he had been elsewhere. However, Thomas was not convinced and replied, 'Unless I see the nail marks in his hands and put my finger where the nails were, and put my hand into his side, I will not believe it' (John 20:25). Eight days later, however, Jesus reappeared; he stood among the disciples and said, 'Peace be with you!' (v. 26). This time Thomas *was* present. Knowing exactly what Thomas had said, Jesus singled him out saying, 'Put your finger here; see my hands. Reach out your hand and put it into my side. Stop doubting and believe' (v. 27).

Thomas said to him, 'My Lord and my God!' (v. 28). Jesus treated Thomas with this special kind of grace; he did not have to do this, but he dealt with his disciples in this very tender way, leading them step by step. However, there came a time when these disciples did not need to be convinced at the human level of understanding. After the Day of Pentecost, when the Holy Spirit descended upon them, Jesus was even more real to them than he had been when he lived among them, and the one who made the difference was the Holy Spirit.

This is still the case. Some hear the gospel message, several times perhaps, without being convinced of the claims of Christianity. They say, 'I have listened to the arguments, and I think I have been very fair. I have heard enough to decide that its claims are untrue.' They believe that Christianity is something that they grasp with their powers of reasoning, but Christianity is not like that. Christianity is convincing only when the Holy Spirit penetrates people's hearts, and when that happens, they are never the same again. Then what amazes them most is that they have not understood the gospel before.

It is interesting that the Bible has a good deal to say about the hands of God. For example, it sometimes refers to God's hands in terms of his anger. Exodus 8 says:

> Then the LORD said to Moses, 'Tell Aaron, "Stretch out your staff and strike the dust of the ground, and throughout the land of Egypt the dust will become gnats."' They did this, and when Aaron stretched out his hand with the staff and struck the dust of the ground, gnats came upon men and animals. All the dust throughout the land of Egypt became gnats. But when the magicians tried to produce gnats by their secret arts, they could not. And the gnats were on men and animals.
>
> The magicians said to Pharaoh, 'This is the finger of God.'

But Pharaoh's heart was hard and he would not listen, just as the Lord had said (vv. 16–19).

Let me give you another example. In 1 Samuel 4:10–11 we read:

So the Philistines fought, and the Israelites were defeated and every man fled to his tent. The slaughter was very great; Israel lost thirty thousand foot soldiers. The ark of God was captured.

Then word went round that the hand of God was heavy upon them.

The expression 'the right hand of God', often used in terms of God's anger, is also used in terms of his power and his keeping grace. God's powerful hand keeps those who are his. Jesus said, 'I give them eternal life, and they shall never perish; no-one can snatch them out of my hand' (John 10:28). Paul reminded Timothy of the security Christians enjoy when he wrote to him, saying 'God's solid foundation stands firm, sealed with this inscription: "The Lord knows those who are his"' (2 Tim. 2:19). Paul could also say in his letter to the Philippians, 'He who began a good work in you will carry it on to completion until the day of Christ Jesus' (Phil. 1:6).

So if the Holy Spirit arrests you, you may be assured that God is not going to save you only to reject you later. The hand God uses to arouse you or to warn you will be the hand that will keep you. If you truly turn to Jesus and he saves you, you will be a child of God for ever. He will *never* let you go.

Are you a backslider? Do you feel that Jesus has rejected you because of something you have done? Perhaps you have wandered away from him; you have done things that you ought not to have done, and you no longer have the joy, the peace and the rest that you once knew. Maybe your life is in turmoil, and you wonder whether there is any hope and, above all, you question whether Jesus *ever* loved you. Listen: you are still a child of God and Jesus will not let anything or anyone snatch you from his hand. But he asks you now to return to him and to repent. He will forgive you. Then let him shape your past; let him restore to you the joy of your salvation. Paul said that nothing 'will be able to separate us from the love of God that is in Christ Jesus our Lord' (Rom. 8:39). The wonderful thing about Jesus' hands is that he uses them not only as a sign of his power and a sign of his anger, but also as a sign of his mercy and love.

Yet Revelation refers not merely to the hands of Jesus, but specifically to his *right* hand. I do not think this is incidental. We use this word 'right' in many ways. We can use it in terms of correctness: whether someone is right or wrong. We use it in terms of direction: whether we go to the right or to the left. Moreover, as we all know, it deals with one's ideology, whether politically or theologically one is on the right or on the left. However, when we speak of the right hand of God, it does not indicate where God stands politically. In Scripture the expression 'the right hand of God' is used explicitly. I will show you three ways.

First, the right hand of God denotes a place of exceeding joy. In Psalm 16:11 David concluded that God would fill him 'with joy in your presence, with eternal pleasures at your right hand'.

The second thing I would say about the right hand of God is that it is the place to which Christ has been exalted. On the Day of Pentecost, Peter, after referring to Psalm 16, put it like this:

'God has raised this Jesus to life, and we are all witnesses of the fact. Exalted to the right hand of God, he has received from the Father the promised Holy Spirit and has poured out what you now see and hear. For David did not ascend to heaven, and yet he said,

"The Lord said to my Lord:
  'Sit at my right hand
until I make your enemies
  a footstool for your feet"' (Acts 2:32-35).

The third use of the expression is that it denotes the position of Christians on the Day of Judgment. Jesus said:

'When the Son of Man comes in his glory, and all the angels with him, he will sit on his throne in heavenly glory. All the nations will be gathered before him, and he will separate the people one from another as a shepherd separates the sheep from the goats. He will put the sheep on his right and the goats on his left' (Matt. 25:31-33).

Thus you see the threefold significance in Scripture of the term 'the right hand of God.' It is (1) the place where supreme joy is found at God's right hand, (2) the place to which Jesus has been exalted, and (3) your position on Judgment Day if you recognize you are a sinner and accept the salvation Jesus offers.

The Bible tells us John had a glimpse of Jesus. 'His face', said John 'was like the sun shining in all its brilliance. When I saw him, I fell at his feet as though dead. Then he placed his right hand on me' (Rev. 1:16–17). If God ever lets you know that his right hand is upon you that means that he is telling you how it is going to be with you on Judgment Day. Matthew 25:34 tells us what will happen: 'Then the King will say to those on his right, "Come, you who are blessed by my Father; take your inheritance, the kingdom prepared for you since the creation of the world."' You can never hear any better news than this, and if God puts his right hand on you now, you may be sure you will be on his right hand then.

But not only that, when the Lord lays his right hand upon you, it means that he has exalted you to be a co-heir with Jesus Christ (Rom. 8:17). Now this thought is so extraordinary that I dare not say much. It means that the Father will love and protect you in the way he loves his own Son. Moreover, in the same way God has exalted his Son to his right hand, so he will exalt you with him. This is amazing, but that is how much God loves those who honour his Son.

Furthermore, if the Lord sets his right hand upon you, he is giving you the foundation for the greatest joy in the world. You may have thought that joy is in worldly pleasure, in sex, in drugs, in alcohol, in gambling, in drinking and in immoral living. No. That joy is fleeting and only adds to your guilt, unless you succeed in so repressing it that you have a dulled conscience. Instead, come to see that if the Lord puts his right hand on you, he is granting you real joy – the joy of knowing forgiveness, the joy of being free of guilt, the joy of knowing your eternal destination. That is the gospel.

Finally, do you recall that Jesus had seven stars in his right hand? Revelation 1 tells us they mean the ministers of God are in Christ's right hand. It is another way of saying that you will receive the touch of his right hand only through Christians who share the gospel with you. Now you may say, 'I don't need a preacher; I will deal with God myself.' But remember, Paul said, 'It pleased God by the foolishness of preaching to save them that believe' (1 Cor. 1:21, AV). Take this seriously. On Judgment Day Jesus will say this to those on his left hand, 'Depart from me, you who are cursed, into the eternal fire prepared for the devil and his angels.' (Matt. 25:41).

Jesus reaches out his right hand to touch the weary, the guilty and the backslider. He says, 'Turn around. Come to me; follow me and find eternal joy.'

27

The Touch of Jesus

Revelation 1:17

Perhaps the most magnificent subject I have ever dealt with is 'The Touch of Jesus'. It gives hope to any who are discouraged, lonely or troubled. The touch of Jesus is all that is needed to turn around the most hopeless situation. I say that without the slightest exaggeration. This is something that is attested – not only by God's word, but also by experience. You may say, 'But you don't know my situation.' That is true, but I know what the touch of Jesus can do. You do not need more psychological help, you do not need more education, you do not need more money; you simply need to feel his touch.

But the person John saw was not the 'popular' Jesus of whom you have heard. John just had a glimpse of Jesus and he was overcome. In Revelation 1:17 John describes what happened to him like this: 'When I saw him, I fell at his feet as though dead.' The 'popular' Jesus, if he existed, would have no power to knock you down.

Millions have no conception of who Jesus is. They picture Jesus as a man who once died on a cross. I will tell you about someone like that. Saul of Tarsus (later to become the apostle Paul) was convinced that not only was Jesus an impostor but that his followers were doing great harm. He believed that ridding the world of Christians would be to do it a favour. Saul was a realist. He was not worried about

Jesus, because the Jesus he knew about was the same Jesus who is popular today – the one who has *not* risen from the tomb. The Jesus who enraged Saul was dead. He sincerely believed that the reports that Jesus was alive were idle tales and that persecuting Christians would prevent them spreading this gossip. But then, Saul had an experience that took him completely by surprise. He could never have anticipated that one day when he was on the road to Damascus, a bright light would shine in his path, knocking him down and that he would hear Jesus speak to him (Acts 9:1–9). His experience was very similar to John's. Several hundred years earlier the prophet Isaiah also shared this kind of experience. He too was struck down, and when he saw the glory of God, he was concerned about his sinful condition and cried out, 'Woe to me!' (Isa. 6:5). So what happened to John when he said, 'I fell at his feet as though dead' was not a novel experience: it had happened before – and it has happened since. What restored John was that Jesus put his right hand on him and said, 'Do not be afraid. I am the First and the Last' (v. 17). He needed the *touch*.

The idea of touch fascinates many people. In recent years a certain kind of group therapy, where people sit in a circle and touch each other, sometimes blindfolded, has become popular. It is supposed to make people feel closer to one another and free them from their inhibitions.

Some people think that touching somebody famous, or even touching something they have handled, is a thrilling experience. I will never forget some years ago, when the Beatles were at the height of their fame, my little sister came to visit us in Fort Lauderdale. She was an ardent Beatles' fan and, when she discovered that the group had stayed at a certain hotel in Miami Beach a few weeks earlier, she wanted to see it. So I drove her down to the hotel. 'Please, RT, let's go in,' she begged. Once we were inside, she asked the head porter which room had been theirs. 'Let me have a look,' she pleaded. So we took the lift upstairs and found the room in which the group had stayed. On the door was the room number. My sister simply wanted to touch it. That was all it took to satisfy her – a touch.

That is what will solve your problem – one touch. Do you sometimes feel that you are always left out but if you sit around waiting nothing will ever happen? Some people in the Bible felt like that, and rather than wait for Jesus to come to them, they went to him. If you have a problem and you are determined to find Jesus, don't wait for him to come to you; search for him and discover where he is.

Now we know where Jesus has *been*. He was born in Bethlehem and grew up in Nazareth, a town in the northern part of Galilee. Then, when he was about thirty years old, John baptized him in the River Jordan. After this, for the next three years this man Jesus went around doing unusual things: touching people, healing them and allowing them to reach out in faith and touch him. Yet only three years later he was crucified.

No one had expected something like this to happen. After all, this man had the power to raise the dead. He had the power to control the laws of nature, to calm storms, to enable Peter to walk on the water, to take a few loaves and fishes and multiply them so they fed five thousand people. He had given sight to the blind, cast out demons and performed many other miracles. Who would ever have dreamed that the man who did all that would one day be hanging helplessly on a cross. It did not make sense. Anybody who could do those miraculous things could surely have prevented that happening! People who think like this are right. Jesus could have stopped his crucifixion. Thankfully, he did not because what he did on the cross procured our salvation. The story does not end with Jesus' death. After three days Jesus rose from the dead, and forty days later he ascended to heaven. That is where he is now.

I have some very good news for you. Do you know the way Jesus touches people now? He touches them by using Christians to preach the gospel. If, when you hear the good news, the Holy Spirit falls on you, you will experience his touch; and you will see everything is different. Nothing is worse than to feel your life is in turmoil. But when Jesus touches you, your world is changed and everything is put right. I know this is an extraordinary claim, nevertheless, that is what happens.

You can see why, when Jesus was on this earth, people did not wait for him to come but went to find him. In Matthew's Gospel we read: 'People brought all their sick to him and begged him to let the sick just touch the edge of his cloak, and all who touched him were healed' (Matt 14:35-36).

Now it is a question of how earnest you are about finding Jesus, but if you can reach him he will solve your problems. Do you remember the story of the woman who, for twelve years, had suffered from internal bleeding? (see Chapter 14). Unable to get close enough to speak to Jesus because of the crowds thronging around him, she somehow managed to touch the hem of his cloak and was completely cured (Matt. 9:20-22). Just touching him makes all the difference.

Yet there is another way of touching him, that is by not pretending when you are in his presence. Now if you pretend with other people they may not realize that you are, in fact, wearing a mask. You may say, 'Oh, yes, I wear a mask. Of course I do. I need to project a certain kind of image.' We all do that. We don't want others to know us as we really are lest they reject us. Now you may convince others you are just the most upright citizen, that you have a sound mind and a balanced outlook on life. You can talk to them and they may think you are wonderful; they may be easy to fool. But you won't touch Jesus by wearing a mask. In Hebrews, we read, 'Everything is uncovered and laid bare before the eyes of him to whom we must give account' (Heb. 4:13). Jesus sees you as you are; he is not touched by your contrived demeanour, by your false expression or by words you do not mean. If you want to touch him, stop pretending. It will save much wasted time in his presence.

Yet perhaps somebody is reading this who says, 'I am so desperate; I am frozen with fear. I don't know which way to look or to turn. I don't know *how* to find Jesus.' Then your only hope is that he finds you. But I have good news. He *has* come to find you. Jesus said, '[I] came to seek and to save what was lost' (Luke 19:10). He will find you because he knows where you are. He knows when you were born; he saw you in the cradle. He knew all about you before you could know anything about yourself. Do you know he has been following you through the years?

You may ask, 'What will Jesus do when he finds me?' The answer is, he will deal with you as you are. Moreover, when he comes, he will not scold you or moralize and say, 'Now look, you are in an awful mess; you ought to be ashamed of yourself. Why waste my time when you have got yourself into a state like this?' No. That is how others may treat you, but not Jesus. However, he will wait until you invite him into your life. You see, Jesus treats you courteously. He waits until you *know* that you need him and ask him to touch you.

What happens, then, when Jesus touches you? The first thing that will happen is that you will have a sense of objectivity and see yourself clearly. Until now you have been unable to do this, and perhaps you have blamed others for your problems – your parents, your schoolteacher, the church or the government, but the fault is yours! Yet you do not realize that until Jesus touches you. Then you will feel like Isaiah, who said, 'Woe to me!' (Isa. 6:5) and like Peter, who said, 'Go away from me, Lord; I am a sinful man' (Luke 5:8). You will see yourself in a way you never thought possible. You will see that you have caused your own problems and that the root of your predicament is sin. Jesus' touch makes all the difference. His touch also enables you to view him clearly. You will see the same Jesus Saul of Tarsus saw that day. You will see the same Jesus that John saw. And, like them, you will see that he is alive and realize his death on the cross was the best thing that could possibly happen.

The understanding you receive will be twofold. First, you will realize that you need Jesus as your Saviour because you can never deal with the problem of sin. Jesus died for all your sins – the sins that haunt you and burden you with guilt. Don't try to punish yourself by doing better; don't try to compete with what Jesus did. Just recognize you need a Saviour and he has done everything for you. The wonderful thing is that what Jesus did on the cross is complete; you cannot add to it. Next, you will see that you need Jesus as your Lord and that you must submit your life to his control.

The third thing that will happen when Jesus touches you is that your guilt will disappear and healing will begin. Yet the most extraordinary thing is this: Jesus then has the responsibility (remember this) for shaping your past. 'The past has gone,' you may say. 'How can he possibly do anything about that?' I don't understand it – but he does! He has a way of stepping in and his touch changes your whole world, and the longer you live, the more you will see that

Jesus always had his hand on your life and that he was following you, waiting for you to come to him.

His touch makes all the difference. Have you experienced that touch? Do you remember the leper who said, 'Lord, if you are willing, you can make me clean' (Matt. 8:2)? Jesus replied, 'I am willing' (v. 3). Then he touched him and immediately the leprosy was gone. Let Jesus touch you. His touch will make you whole.

Christian Focus Publications publishes biblically-accurate books for adults and children. The books in the adult range are published in three imprints.

Christian Heritage contains classic writings from the past.

Christian Focus contains popular works including biographies, commentaries, doctrine, and Christian living.

Mentor focuses on books written at a level suitable for Bible College and seminary students, pastors, and others; the imprint includes commentaries, doctrinal studies, examination of current issues, and church history.

For a free catalogue of all our titles, please write to
Christian Focus Publications,
Geanies House, Fearn,
Ross-shire, IV20 1TW, Great Britain

For details of our titles visit us on our web site
http://www.christianfocus.com

R T Kendall is the pastor of Westminster Chapel, London where he is engaged in a much-appreciated Bible teaching ministry. He is a regular speaker at conventions, including Spring Harvest and Keswick.

He has also written over a dozen books and in addition to this book Christian Focus Publications have previously published five of his titles.

Meekness and Majesty is an exposition of Philippians 2:5-11 where Paul deals with the humility of Jesus in his earthly life and the glory of his present heavenly position. R.T. gives a lucid and heartwarming explanation of this well-known passage of Scripture. Derick Bingham says of *Meekness and Majesty*: 'This book exalts the Lord Jesus in everything it says. Reading it will aid you to do the same.'
ISBN 1 871676 87 8   224 pages   pocket paperback

When God Says Well Done is an examination of the various details found in 1 Corinthians concerning the future judgement of believers by Christ when he returns. R.T. is convinced that Paul teaches that the lives of believers will be thoroughly reviewed by their Master who will reward those who served him well. However, there will be loss of reward for those believers who do not serve their Saviour as they could have. In this book, R.T. urges believers to live so as to please God and be commended by Jesus on the Day of Judgment.
ISBN 1 85792 017 1   224 pages B format

Are You Stone Deaf to the Spirit or Rediscovering God is R.T's way of explaining the persons described in Hebrews 5:11-6:12. Chapter 6:4-8 has worried many Christians since it seems to teach that believers can lose their salvation. Dr Kendall gained helpful insights into the teachings of the Book of Hebrews during the eleven years he preached through the book as part of the regular weekly ministry in Westminster Chapel. He believes the passage is describing true believers who have backslidden to a very marked extent, reaching the stage where they have become deaf to God's voice. However, he also finds much in the passage to encourage Christians to renew their commitment to Jesus, particularly God's oath of commitment to all his people.
ISBN 1 85792 072 4 224 pages large format

Higher Ground is a devotional treatment of the Psalms of Degrees (121-134) that were sung by Jewish pilgrims during their visits to Jerusalem to celebrate the annual feasts. R.T. takes one thought from each psalm and applies it helpfully to Christian living today.
ISBN 1 85792 158 5 176 pages pocket paperback

Understanding Theology examines 53 important doctrines of the Christian Faith. They were originally delivered on Friday nights at Westminster Chapel as part of RT's School of Theology. The outline format of the original lectures has been retained. Doctrines explained include

HOW DOES GOD MAKE HIMSELF KNOWN?,
INTERPRETING THE BIBLE,
THE TRINITY,

THE SOVEREIGNTY OF GOD,
THE CROSS OF CHRIST,
THE RESURRECTION OF JESUS,
THE ATONEMENT,
THE ASCENSION OF JESUS,
THE BELIEVER'S POSITION 'IN CHRIST'
JUSTIFICATION BY FAITH
THE BAPTISM OF THE HOLY SPIRIT
THE WORSHIP OF GOD
THE PRIESTHOOD OF ALL BELIEVERS
THE ROLE OF WOMEN IN MINISTRY
BEARING THE CROSS
APOSTASY AND BACKSLIDING
THE JUDGEMENT SEAT OF CHRIST
REWARDS IN HEAVEN
WHAT HAPPENS TO THE LOST?

Hardback 448 pages ISBN 1 85792 429 0